Annual Editions: Early Childhood Education, 37/e

Karen Menke Paciorek

http://create.mheducation.com

ISBN-10: 1260196941   ISBN-13: 9781260196948

Contents

Detailed Table of Contents

Unit 1: Building a Strong Foundation

Kindergartners Get Little Time to Play. Why Does It Matter? Christopher Brown, *The Conversation*, 2016
Forty years ago legendary early childhood educator Jimmy Hymes called it the dribble down disease, the practice of pushing down the curriculum from first grade to kindergarten. It's not that the curriculum is more academic than it was in the past, it is the removal of opportunities to freely explore, create and test out hypothesis that are causing great concern. Children need ample time to engage in activities that foster the academics.

Head Start: A Bridge from Past to Future, Blythe S.F. Hinitz, *Young Children*, 2014
Head Start celebrated its 50th anniversary in the summer of 2014. We can learn from this historic program and the work done across the country to help families in poverty and their children at-risk of future success in school.

Running a Pre-K Program Is Hard. So Why Do Some States Require Almost No Qualifications? Abbie Lieberman and Laura Bornfreund, *Slate.com*, 2017
Administering a building where care and education take place for young children unable to verbally communicate their needs is different in many ways from the role of a K-12 building principal, yet very similar in many other ways. Staff evaluations, managing the physical environment and communicating with families are all job responsibilities in both settings. However those responsible for early childhood settings are required to have far fewer qualifications and often receive compensation much lower than the K-12 setting.

Play Is the Way . . ., Stuart Brown and Kristen Cozad, *SGI Quarterly*, 2013
Despite the overwhelming and very striking research on the benefits of play on current and future learning for children, there are those who argue play time is wasted time. The authors describe characteristics; they call signatures, which indicate an activity is play. They also point to the evidence that people of all ages who are allowed to engage in freely chosen play are more creative and productive. Those focused solely on academic achievement would do well to read the research on the benefits of play in all areas of development. Early childhood educators must advocate for adequate play opportunities for all children.

The Importance of Equal Pay between Pre-K and K-3rd Teachers, Anna Sillers, New *America*, 2017
Teachers working with young children in state funded Pre-K programs earn on average 80p percent of what Kindergarten teachers receive in the same community. The inequity of compensation in early childhood education is a significant issue that affects the profession. All teachers deserve to be compensates appropriately.

6 Policies to Support the Early Childhood Workforce, Rebecca Ullrich, Katie Hamm, and Leila Schochet, *Center for American Progress*, 2017
Working in early childhood education is one of the lowest paying, least respected but most needed professions according to multiple surveys. There are policies that would assist those who spend their days caring for and educate our youngest learners. They include, developing a comprehensive professional development system, move toward parity with kindergarten teachers for compensation and benefits, and provide scholarships and rewards to make earning professional degrees attainable.

The Hell of American Day Care: An Investigation into the Barely Regulated, Unsafe Business of Looking After Our Children, Jonathan Cohn, *The New Republic*, 2013
Ask any soon-to-be or working parent what concerns they have about the pending birth and often the number one concern centers on childcare. Finding and paying for quality child care hangs heavy on the mind of parents. Licensing rules vary significantly from state to state and as a country we have made little progress over the years to help parents make wise choices for the care and education of their most precious possession in a safe and stimulating environment.

Unit 2: Supporting the Development of Young Children and Their Families

Making the Right Choice Simple: Selecting Materials for Infants and Toddlers, Ani N. Shabazian and Caroline Li Soga, *Young Children*, 2014
Providing the appropriate toys and materials for exploration and play by infants and toddlers is critical. The health and safety of

American children are suspended each year. Educators need to be aware of the data and develop effective and appropriate guidance practices that will best serve all young children but especially those in private preschools with an expulsion rate double that of pubic preschools.

Teach Up for Excellence, Carol Ann Tomlinson and Edwin Lou Javius, *Educational Leadership*, 2012
The phrase "engage their minds" is a powerful reminder to all teachers of what we need to do to foster the love of and joy in learning. Setting the academic achievement bar high and then providing the support and services to help diverse learners achieve is one of the most important jobs for a teacher. The authors provide principles for teaching up to afford all students, especially those at-risk, the opportunities to learn in an excellent environment.

Response to Intervention and Early Childhood Best Practices: Working Hand in Hand So All Children Can Learn, Karen Wise Lindeman, *Young Children*, 2013
Teachers of all levels of children must be familiar with Response to Intervention tiers and the strategies to prevent future failure. When educators look for ways to differentiate the learning so every child can learn, success will happen. Resources for additional information are also included.

Unit 5: Practices that Help Children Thrive in School

Quality 101: Identifying the Core Components of a High-quality Early Childhood Program, Simon Workman and Rebecca Ullrich, Center for American Progress, 2017
Choosing childcare is one of the most complicated tasks parents face. Understanding the components of high-quality care and navigating the many types of programs available require knowledge of how children best learn and the qualities necessary in those who care for and educate young children.

It's Play Time! Joan Almon, *Principal*, 2013
There exists great discrepancy between what researchers know are best practices for children and what actually happens in schools and classrooms. The importance of play-based learning is well-documented, yet informed administrators, teachers, and parents work tirelessly to spread the work about the importance of allowing children of all ages quality time to play.

Good Thinking! Fostering Children's Reasoning and Problem Solving, Jessica Vick Whittaker, *Young Children*, 2014
New research on cognitive development and how children develop critical thinking skills is resonating with teachers. Inquiry-based learning experiences in the classroom allow children to develop the necessary problem-solving skills for approaching future learning. These practices can be developmentally appropriate and important to the early childhood curriculum.

10 Ways Kindergarten Can Stop Failing Our Kids, Laurie Levy, *AlterNet*, 2014
There is great discrepancy between what actually happens in kindergartens and what should happen in a child-centered kindergarten based on our knowledge of child development and best practices for five year olds. Teachers need to be strong advocates for the learning styles of the children in their class. Levy provides a specific list of 10 developmentally appropriate practices.

Supporting Children's Learning While Meeting State Standards, Lisa S. Goldstein and Michelle Bauml, *Young Children*, 2012
Teachers are professional decision makers supporting their students' learning with daily decisions concerning classroom activities and lessons. Goldstein and Bauml suggest three traits necessary for teachers to balance the needs of the students and the rigorous demand of state standards and district-mandated curriculum.

Time to Play: Recognizing the Benefits of Recess, Catherine Ramstetter and Robert Murray, *American Educator*, 2017
According to research by the CDC only 54 percent of educators are prohibited from using recess as a privilege to be earned based on appropriate behavior leaving children in other classrooms to be denied the opportunity to engage in free play due to their lack of work completion or behavior. The American Academy of Pediatrics recommends at least 60 minutes of active play each day. That is most often obtained during recess time. Many believe recess is a waste of time that could be better used in direct instruction.

Let's Get Messy! Exploring Sensory and Art Activities with Infants and Toddlers, Trudi Schwarz and Julia Luckenbill, *Young Children*, 2012
Schwarz and Luckenbill include over a dozen possible creative play-based activities for adults to plan for infants and toddlers to engage them in diverse sensorial experiences and list many materials that can easily be collected. A discussion about adults being culturally sensitive in the materials offered to young children is also included.

Time for Play, Stephanie Hanes, *The Christian Science Monitor*, 2012
Defending the benefits of play and the importance of children having access to learning experiences that allow for active learning is an ongoing challenge for early childhood educators who follow best practice. Development in all areas including social and emotional, physical, cognitive, and creative can be achieved through freely chosen play.

Happy 100th Birthday, Unit Blocks! Karyn W. Tunks, *Young Children*, 2013
Long been a staple in quality early childhood programs; the sturdy and reliable unit block is 100 years old. Known as a must have material by most teachers the opportunities for creative, cognitive, physical, and social skills to develop by participating in block play are endless. Blocks, other than the 100 year-old unit block, are described along with the importance of block play.

Animal Attraction: Including Animals in Early Childhood Classrooms, Clarissa M. Uttley, *Young Children*, 2013
The decision to include animals in an early childhood classroom should not be made lightly. Teachers must be committed to the care of the animal throughout the year and incorporate the animal into the daily activities of the classroom. Family concerns and allergies must be taken into consideration along with the access to animals the children may have in their homes and community. The author includes many points to aid the teacher in making the decision.

Food Allergy Concerns in Primary Classrooms: Keeping Children Safe, Peggy Thelen and Elizabeth Ann Cameron, *Young Children*, 2012
Thelen and Cameron provide a comprehensive overview for primary grade teachers and other school personnel to provide a food safe environment. It begins with staff knowledgeable about eating behaviors, specific allergies, and how to recognize and respond to an emergency due to exposure to allergens. Staff should work to establish a safe environment for all.

Unit 6: Curricular Issues

Starting Out Practices to Use in K-3, Nell K. Duke, *Educational Leadership*, 2013
The Common Core State Standards are changing the way teachers teach reading. Gone are the materials comprised of mostly fiction with cute sounding names like Flossie Flamingo replaced instead with more informational text. Teachers must make their classrooms informational text rich and provide multiple opportunities for early literacy experiences to inform as well as entertain.

Social Studies in Preschool? Yes! Ann S. Epstein, *Young Children*, 2014
Social Studies is one curricular content area that is often neglected in the early childhood classroom. Epstein explains the importance of children developing a sense of community and who they are during the preschool years. Teaching strategies are included to assist the teacher in implementing appropriate practices.

Every Child, Every Day, Richard L. Allington and Rachael E. Gabriel, *Educational Leadership*, 2012
Six research-based elements of literacy instruction that will ensure high-quality instructional activities for all students, every day are described. A student's personal choice is a key to the effectiveness of these elements even for struggling readers.

Preface

In publishing ANNUAL EDITIONS, we recognize the enormous role played by the magazines, newspapers, and journals of the public press in providing current, first-rate educational information in a broad spectrum of interest areas. Many of these articles are appropriate for students, researchers, and professionals seeking accurate, current material to help bridge the gap between principles and theories and the real world. These articles, however, become more useful for study when those of lasting value are carefully collected, organized, indexed, and reproduced in a low-cost format, which provides easy and permanent access when the material is needed. That is the role played by ANNUAL EDITIONS.

Annual Editions: Early Childhood Education has evolved during the 40 years it has been in existence to become one of the most used texts for students in early childhood education. This annual collection of the best relevant articles is used today at over 550 colleges and universities. In addition, it may be found in public libraries, pediatricians' offices, and teacher reference sections of school libraries. As the editor for 34 of the 40 years, I work diligently to find articles and bring you the best and most significant readings in the field. I realize this is a tremendous responsibility to provide a thorough review of the current literature—a responsibility I take very seriously. I am always on the lookout for possible articles for the next *Annual Editions: Early Childhood Education*. My goal is to provide the reader with a snapshot of the critical issues facing professionals in early childhood education. The overviews for each unit describe in more detail the issues related to the unit topic and provide the reader with additional information about the issues. I encourage everyone to read the short, but useful unit overviews prior to reading the articles.

Early childhood education is an interdisciplinary field that includes child development, family issues, educational practices, behavior guidance, and curriculum. *Annual Editions: Early Childhood Education 37th edition* brings you the latest information in the field from a wide variety of recent journals, newspapers, online sites, and magazines.

There are four themes found in the readings chosen for this 37th edition of *Annual Editions: Early Childhood Education*. As the editor I read a preponderance of articles on four key issues. They are the:

(1) importance of adults developing a personal relationship to foster social and emotional development with each child as well as their family members and other adults.
(2) key role educators play in supporting hands on exploratory play-based learning activities for all children, but especially our youngest learners.
(3) low public perception of teachers and administrators in Early Childhood Education and the unsatisfactory level of compensation received compared to K-12 educators.
(4) effects of media technology on a variety of developmental domains.

As I read the many articles for consideration I viewed them from my role as a grandmother to now three-year-old Davis and how his absolutely terrific parents are navigating parenting in the world today. Challenges abound but armed with solid research they are raising a caring, curious, and thoughtful boy. They are fortunate for after searching they found a high-quality family childcare home where the owner, Michelle Rozenbeck, recognizes the critical role she plays in the lives of the children in her care. My wish is all young children would have someone like Miss Michelle in their lives that they eagerly run to in the morning and wonder what exciting explorations await for them that day.

It is especially gratifying to see issues affecting children and families addressed in magazines other than professional association journals. The general public needs to be aware of the impact of positive early learning and family experiences on the growth and development of children. There are also numerous websites and other online sources which are adding to our ever expanding collection of knowledge about the development of young children.

Readers are encouraged to explore the Internet sites provided with each article on their own or in collaboration with others for extended learning opportunities. All of these sites were carefully reviewed by university students for their worthiness and direct application to those who work with young children on a day-to-day basis.

Given the wide range of topics; *Annual Editions: Early Childhood Education 37th edition* may be used by several groups—undergraduate or graduate students, professionals, parents, or administrators who want to develop an understanding of the critical issues in the field.

I appreciate the time the advisory board members take to provide suggestions for improvement and possible articles for consideration. The production and editorial staff of McGraw-Hill, led by Mary Foust, ably support and coordinate the efforts to publish this book.

I look forward to hearing from you about the selection of articles and especially value correspondence from students who take the time to share their thoughts on the profession or articles selected. Comments and articles sent for consideration are welcomed and will serve to modify future volumes. I encourage you to follow my semi-regular thoughts and updates on the Early Childhood Education profession on twitter @karenpaciorek or contact me at kpaciorek@emich.edu.

Karen Menke Paciorek
Eastern Michigan University

Editor of This Volume

KAREN MENKE PACIOREK is a professor and coordinator of Early Childhood Education and Children and Families programs at Eastern Michigan University in Ypsilanti. Her degrees in early childhood education include a BA from the University of Pittsburgh, an MA from George Washington University and a PhD from Peabody College of Vanderbilt University. She is the editor of Taking Sides: Clashing Views in Early Childhood Education (2nd ed.) also published by McGraw-Hill. She has served as a president of the Michigan Association for the Education of Young Children, the Michigan Early Childhood Education Consortium, and the Northville Board of Education. She presents at local, state, and national conferences on curriculum planning, guiding behavior, preparing the learning environment, and working with families. She served for nine years as a member of the Board of Education for the Northville Public Schools, Northville, Michigan. She is currently on the Board of Trustees for the Eastern Michigan University Foundation, Women in Philanthropy at EMU, Wolverine Human Services Detroit, MI, and the Neonatal Intensive Care Unit at St. Joseph Mercy Hospital Ann Arbor, MI. Dr. Paciorek is a recipient of the Eastern Michigan University Distinguished Faculty Award for Service and the Outstanding Teaching Award from the Alumni Association.

Academic Advisory Board

Members of the Academic Advisory Board are instrumental in the final selection of articles for the *Annual Editions* series. Their review of the articles for content, level, and appropriateness provides critical direction to the editor(s)

and staff. We think that you will find their careful consideration reflected in this book.

Carlene Henderson
Sam Houston State University

Shelli Henehan
University of Arkansas, Fort Smith

Dana Hilbert
Cameron University

Alice S. Honig
Syracuse University

Christy Hopkins
Stanly Community College

Glenda Hotton
Masters College

Joan Packer Isenberg
George Mason University

Richard T. Johnson
University of Hawaii, Manoa

Lois Johnson
Grove City College

Dr. C. Morrell Jones
University of Arkansas Monticello

Carol Karian
Fullerton College

Katharine C. Kersey
Old Dominion University

Sherry King
University of South Carolina

Michelle Larocque
Florida Atlantic University, Boca Raton

Dennis A. Lichty
Wayne State College

Miranda Lin
Illinois State University

Leanna Manna
Villa Maria College

Michael Martinsen
Edgewood College

John W. McNeeley
Daytona State College

Charlotte Metoyer
National Louis University

Gayle Mindes
DePaul University

George S. Morrison
University of North Texas

William A. Mosier
Wright State University

Barbie Norvell
Coastal Carolina University

Caroline Olko
Nassau Community College

Christine Pack
Westmoreland County Community College

Jessie Panko
Saint Xavier University

Karen L. Peterson
Washington State University

Peter Phipps
Dutchess Community College

Laura Pierce
University of West Alabama

Jack V. Powell
University of Georgia

Frankie Denise
Powell   University of North Carolina, Pembroke

Frank Prerost
Midwestern University

Anne Marie Rakip
Palm Beach State College

Mary Eva Repass
University of Virginia

Greer Richardson
La Salle University

Claire N. Rubman
Suffolk County Community College

Jana Sanders
Texas A & M University, Corpus Christi

Thomas R. Scheira
Buffalo State College

Stephen T. Schroth
Knox College

Hilary Seitz
University of Alaska, Anchorage

LaShorage Shaffer
University of Michigan, Dearborn

Laura Shea Doolan
Molloy College

Paulette Shreck
University of Central Oklahoma

Wallace Smith
Union County College

Dolores Stegelin
Clemson University

Unit 1

UNIT

Prepared by: Karen Menke Paciorek, *Eastern Michigan University*

Building a Strong Foundation

The title for this unit "Building a Strong Foundation" is representative of the work we do with our youngest learners and their families. Any builder will tell you if you want a structure to stand for many years, even centuries, you must initially do significant foundation and preparation work before the first stone, steel beam, or load of concrete is set. Shoddy construction will not last and will only lead to more problems in the years to come. The same holds true when planning for the care and education of young children. The articles in this unit all point to the importance of quality Pre-K programs for developing necessary learning skills, closing the achievement gap, and advocating for early childhood education. This unit also broadens the job description of anyone in the profession from one who cares for and educates young children to one who educates family and community members about our field, advocates for our profession, and works to be an informed professional who takes responsibility for the work we do. In short, we are in a profession, not just a job which is performed during specific work hours and then forgotten about when not at work. The early childhood profession requires you to be alert and focused on the field at all times.

I continuously read multiple articles each year on the benefits of play in my search for the best articles for inclusion in this anthology. On one hand, I want to say, "Really, do we still need to tell people about the importance of play?" But I know the message is not being heard by large numbers of individuals. Play has been called as important to our survival as other basic needs such as nutrition or sleep. I wonder why our message about the many benefits of play and the deep need for all children to have multiple opportunities throughout each and every day to engage in freely chosen creative play is not being heard. The play children need is different from playing video games or playing an organized game. This play is what is necessary for developing skills creatively, socially, cognitively, physically, and emotionally; in short, developing the whole child. Please join me in becoming a strong advocate for play in formal educational settings as well as in homes and communities. Educators who are pushing young children to learn in ways that are not developmentally appropriate and which rob them of their special time to learn by manipulating materials and engaging in active play need educating about how children best learn. We should not

have to build a case for play in programs serving young children but should instead be able to foster and support the play in which children engage and help them learn. James L. Hymes, Jr. is one of my favorite early childhood educators from the past century. Dr. Hymes was the director of the Kaiser Ship Yards Child Service Centers in Portland, Oregon, from 1943 to 1945 during World War II and on the initial planning committee for Head Start in 1965. In 1959, he wrote about play in the following way:

> "We need a new word to sum up what young children do with themselves—how they occupy their time, what they give themselves to, the activity that is the be-all and the end-all of their days. We have words to say all this for other ages. We can talk about adults and say that they are 'working.' That sounds right and reasonable. We can talk about the elementary or high school or college age and say that they are 'studying.' That is a dignified description that sounds legitimate and right for the age. But we say that young children 'play.' That is the reason for our schools: to let this age do what it has to do, with more depth and richness, to let these children play. But to many people the word sounds weak and evasive, as if somehow this age was cheating. If we say 'free play' we put two bad words together. Free and soft, and easy, casual, careless, sloppy, pointless, aimless, wandering, senseless. Play of pleasure and ease and waste and evil. The words do violence to the deeds. Can't we find a word or coin a word that conveys the respect this time in life deserves? Must we always minimize it, or hasten it, or deny it?" (Hymes, *The Grade Teacher*, 1959)

It will send chills down your spine if you have ever looked for childcare or worry about undertaking that task in the future. Licensing rules are very different from state to state and budget-short states are sending fewer inspectors out to growing caseloads with shorter visits to homes and childcare centers each year. There is a crisis waiting around every corner and parents must be vigilant when looking for quality care for their children.

With more and more focus on the importance of providing high-quality Pre-K programs, the issue of pay equality for those teaching four-year-olds versus five-year-old kindergarteners is critical. When there is great disparity between the two age levels in pay and other benefits, preschool classrooms are often staffed with a revolving door of teachers who are constantly leaving preschool for higher paying jobs in K-12 classrooms. Supporting staff working with young children is a critical need in all areas. All teachers are dependent on the quality of education children receive during their preschool years. Teachers should not have to work a second job to earn more than the poverty level if they spend their days working with young children.

There are always exceptions to each argument where outstanding academic achievement is found in schools located in extreme poverty areas. The many barriers that prevent children from coming to school each day well rested and fed do affect academic performance and teachers who are aware of the many stumbling blocks children and their families must overcome prior to entering the classroom are better prepared to assist them in their work to achieve in school. Legislators across the country are addressing these gaps in a number of ways. Some states offer universal preschool which is free and available for all preschool children living in that state. Other states are taking a different approach and targeting specific state-funded preschool programs for those children who need and would benefit from preschool the most. This need is often determined by a child meeting two or more risk factors such as a low-income family, a non-English speaking family, a speech, language or hearing deficit, a teenage parent, and so on. There are pros and cons to each approach and this issue will continue to play out in state capitols across the country as they look for the most effective way to help all children succeed.

One of the classes this editor teaches as part of a load as a professor of Early Childhood Education at Eastern Michigan University is a graduate class titled: "Trends, Issues and Advocacy in ECE." In that class, we read writings by many of the individuals who laid the foundation for our profession. John Locke (1632–1704) is one of those individuals. I share with my students a favorite quote Locke wrote back in the mid-1600s "Accommodate the educational program to fit the child; don't change the child to fit the program." That quote is so relevant today as we work to ensure schools are ready for all children.

There is new focus on the individuals who choose a career with young children and their families. Care and education of young children is a profession as defined by the need for initial preparation and ongoing professional development. We must help educators see the importance of ongoing advocacy and professional development and the need to be an active lifelong learner and advocate in the field. Just as we would not want to go to a physician who graduated from medical school over 25 years ago and has never attended a conference or read a professional journal, we would not want that same lack of professional development for our field. We have an added responsibility in our profession since the people with whom we work are unable to speak out for themselves to tell others about the issues they face. The benefits of developing a professional advocacy and development plan are you are able to interact with others who share your passion for the care and education of young children and interaction with their families. It is a wonderful way to build your network of contacts and friends whether you are new to an area or a longtime resident. Get out and get involved in our wonderful profession. Become an active member of a student ECE organization on your campus or start one if none exists. Look to attend professional development opportunities in your community. If funds are available, consider joining a professional organization and contact legislators and educate others who make important decisions that affect our jobs.

I am reminded of one of the more popular perceptions of early care and education held by those outside of the profession. For the past 50 years, "early childhood education was viewed as a panacea the solution to all social ills in society" (Paciorek, 2008, p. xvii). This is huge pressure to put on one profession, especially one that is grossly underpaid. We do have outside forces carefully watching how early education practices affect long-term development and learning. Early childhood professionals must be accountable for practices they implement in their classrooms and how children spend their time interacting with materials. Appropriate early learning standards are the norm in the profession, and knowledgeable caregivers and teachers must be informed of the importance of developing quality experiences that align with the standards and assessment practices. Teachers can no longer plan cute activities that fill the child's days and backpacks with pictures to hang on the refrigerator. Teachers must be intentional in their planning to adapt learning experiences so that all children can achieve standards that are based on knowledge of developmental abilities.

I always feel energized when others outside of the field of early childhood education recognize that quality care and education for young children can have tremendous economic benefits as well as educational benefits for society. Of course we would always welcome the interest from more people outside of the profession, but the field is receiving increased attention from others for a number of reasons. The nation is learning that high-quality programs are beneficial for young children's long-term development. Much of this interest is in part due to some state legislators allocating resources for state-operated preschool programs. Coupled with the knowledge of the importance of ECE programs is a realization that the quality of these programs should be of utmost importance.

As the editor, I hope you benefit from reading the articles and reflecting on the important issues facing early childhood education today. Your job is to share the message with others not familiar with our field about the impact attending a quality program can have on young children throughout their life.

Article   Prepared by: Karen Menke Paciorek, *Eastern Michigan University*

Kindergartners Get Little Time to Play. Why Does It Matter?

CHRISTOPHER BROWN

Learning Outcomes

After reading this article, you will be able to:

- Describe how play helps children academically, socially, and emotionally.
- Advocate for a more balanced approach to instruction.
- Define the importance of social interaction with peers during play.

Being a kindergartner today is very different from being a kindergartner 20 years ago. In fact it is more like first grade.

Researchers have demonstrated that five-year-olds are spending more time engaged in teacher-led academic learning activities than play-based learning opportunities that facilitate child-initiated investigations and foster social development among peers.

As a former kindergarten teacher, a father of three girls who've recently gone through kindergarten, and as researcher and teacher-educator in early childhood education, I have had kindergarten as a part of my adult life for almost 20 years.

As a parent, I have seen how student-led projects, sensory tables (that include sand or water) and dramatic play areas have been replaced with teacher-led instructional time, writing centers and sight words lists that children need to memorize. And as a researcher, I found, along with my colleague Yi Chin Lan, that early childhood teachers expect children to have academic knowledge, social skills, and the ability to control themselves when they enter kindergarten.

So, why does this matter?

All Work, and Almost No Play

First, let's look at what kindergarten looks like today.

As part of my ongoing research, I have been conducting interviews with a range of kindergarten stakeholders—children, teachers, and parents—about what they think kindergarten is and what it should be. During the interviews, I share a 23-min film that I made last spring about a typical day in a public school kindergarten classroom.

The classroom I filmed had 22 kindergartners and one teacher. They were together for almost the entire school day. During that time, they engaged in about 15 different academic activities, which included decoding word drills, practicing sight words, reading to themselves and then to a buddy, counting up to 100 by 1's, 5's, and 10's, practicing simple addition, counting money, completing science activities about living things and writing in journals on multiple occasions. Recess did not occur until last hour of the day, and that too for about 15 min.

For children between the ages of five and six, this is tremendous amount of work. Teachers too are under pressure to cover the material.

When I asked the teacher, who I interviewed for the short film, why she covered so much material in a few hours, she stated,

> There's pressure on me and the kids to perform at a higher level academically.

So even though the teacher admitted that the workload on kindergartners was an awful lot, she also said she was unable to do anything about changing it.

She was required to assess her students continuously, not only for her own instruction but also for multiple assessments such as quarterly report cards, school-based reading

Kindergartners Get Little Time to Play. Why Does It Matter? by Christopher Brown

13

assessments, district-based literacy and math assessments, as well as state-mandated literacy assessments.

In turn, when I asked the kindergartners what they were learning, their replies reflected two things: one, they were learning to follow rules; two, learning was for the sake of getting to the next grade and eventually to find a job. Almost all of them said to me that they wanted more time to play. One boy said:

> I wish we had more recess.

These findings mirror the findings of researchers Daphna Bassok, Scott Latham, and Anna Rorem that kindergarten now focuses on literacy and math instruction. They also echo the statements of other kindergarten teachers that kids are being prepared for high-stakes tests as early as kindergarten.

Here's How Play Helps Children

Research has consistently shown classrooms that offer children the opportunities to engage in play-based and child-centered learning activities help children grow academically, socially, and emotionally. Furthermore, recess in particular helps children restore their attention for learning in the classroom.

Focus on rules can diminish children's willingness to take academic risks and curiosity as well as impede their self-confidence and motivation as learners—all of which can negatively impact their performance in school and in later life.

Giving children a chance to play and engage in hands-on learning activities helps them internalize new information as well as compare and contrast what they're learning with what they already know. It also provides them with the chance to interact with their peers in a more natural setting and to solve problems on their own. Lastly, it allows kindergartners to make sense of their emotional experiences in and out of school.

So children asking for more time to play are not trying to get out of work. They know they have to work in school. Rather, they're asking for a chance to recharge as well as be themselves.

As another kindergarten boy in my study told me,

> We learn about stuff we need to learn, because if we don't learn stuff, then we don't know anything.

Learning by Exploring

So what can we do to help kindergartners?

I am not advocating for the elimination of academics in kindergarten. All of the stakeholders I've talked with up to this point, even the children, know and recognize that kindergartners need to learn academic skills so that they can succeed in school.

However, it is the free exploration that is missing. As a kindergarten teacher I filmed noted:

> Free and exploratory learning has been replaced with sit, focus, learn, get it done, and maybe you can have time to play later.

Policy makers, schools systems, and schools need to recognize that the standards and tests they mandate have altered the kindergarten classroom in significant ways. Families need to be more proactive as well. They can help their children's teachers by being their advocates for a more balanced approach to instruction.

Kindergartners deserve learning experiences in school that nurtures their development as well as their desire to learn and interact with others. Doing so will assist them in seeing school as a place that will help them and their friends be better people.

Critical Thinking

1. Talk to a parent of a child in kindergarten and ask about the play experiences their child has on a daily basis.
2. Observe in a kindergarten classroom and compare what you observed to what you read in the article.

Internet References

It's Playtime—National Association of Elementary School Principals
> https://www.naesp.org/principal-septemberoctober-2013-early-learning/it-s-playtime

Keeping Play in Kindergarten—New America
> https://www.newamerica.org/education-policy/edcentral/kinderplay/

Play and Children's Learning—National Association for the Education of Young Children
> http://www.naeyc.org/play

What Happened to Kindergarten?—Scholastic Teacher
> https://www.scholastic.com/teachers/articles/teaching-content/what-happened-kindergarten/

CHRISTOPHER BROWN is an associate professor of Curriculum and Instruction in Early Childhood Education, University of Texas at Austin.

Brown, Christopher, "Kindergartners Get Little Time to Play: Why Does it Matter?" *The Conversation*, April 27, 2016.

Article Prepared by: Karen Menke Paciorek, *Eastern Michigan University*

Head Start

A Bridge from Past to Future

BLYTHE S.F. HINITZ

Learning Outcomes

After reading this article, you will be able to:

- Articulate the importance of Head Start programs on the development of young children in poverty.

- Advocate for quality Head Start programs for your community.

- Explain why programs related to Head Start were developed and the need they serve.

Head Start was built on a strong base of civil rights advocacy and a long history of private and government-funded US early childhood education programs. At the 50th anniversaries of the Civil Rights Act of 1964 and the Economic Opportunity Act (EOA) of 1964, it is fitting that we remember that Head Start was born of President Lyndon B. Johnson's War on Poverty in the middle of the civil rights movement of the 1960s.

At the time of Head Start's creation, 10 years had already passed since the Supreme Court's momentous *Brown v. Board of Education* (1954) decision that racial segregation in public schools was unconstitutional. The Reverend Dr. Martin Luther King Jr. and others were helping the United States focus on the needs of under-represented groups. President Johnson announced the creation of Head Start in a special message to Congress on January 12, 1965, in which he focused on the expansion of "preschool program[s] in order to reach disadvantaged children early" (Osborn 1991). Lady Bird Johnson launched her role as a national spokeswoman for the Head Start program with a tea in the Rose Garden, attended by members of the Head Start planning committee. The gathering, which was covered on newspaper society pages, gave the program "an aura of respectability" (Kuntz 1998, 8–9).

Varying Views on Head Start

Views varied on what kind of program Head Start should be. It was widely believed at the time that "poverty and welfare dependencies are transmitted intergenerationally [because] . . . education, independence, ambition, [and] concern for the future are not reinforced during a childhood spent in poverty and dependence on welfare" (Washington & Bailey 1995, 21). Those who held this view believed that since parents were accountable for their children's condition, anti-poverty programs—including Head Start—should either remove children from the influence of parents who were not meeting their needs or work to improve the parents for the benefit of the children. This attitude led to the cultural deprivation theory, which "suggested that the poor needed to be educated, to have opportunities to learn the values embraced by middle-class America and that, if introduced to these ideas—most important to the work ethic—the poor would straighten up and act like real Americans" (Kuntz 1998, 4).

Others, believing that parents should personally benefit from a program and that community buy-in was important, suggested a combination of parent education and participation in decision making. Those espousing the least supported view—that poverty is a systemic issue—proposed that parents should be involved in actual program governance.

Although the EOA legislation authorized Community Action Programs (CAPs) to assist local communities in establishing and administering their own antipoverty efforts, some local governments opposed the proposed placement of administrative control and resources in the hands of poor people and refused to apply for program grants. In an effort to make the CAP more palatable to local officials, while using what would have been an embarrassing budget surplus, the Head Start project was born (Zigler & Styfco 1996, 133).

Article   Prepared by: Karen Menke Paciorek, *Eastern Michigan University*

Play Is the Way . . .

Play is not merely a break from useful and productive activities. It is, as Dr. Stuart Brown and Kristen Cozad of the National Institute for Play contend, a fundamental survival drive, as important as adequate nutrition or sleep.

STUART BROWN AND KRISTEN COZAD

Learning Outcomes

After reading this article, you will be able to:

- Advocate for time for daily play for all children.
- Explain to parents the lifelong learning skills developed through play.

What exactly is play? Why did Mother Nature make it so much fun? And what is its purpose when play seems so . . . "purposeless"?

Scientists from many different disciplines are now beginning to understand the importance of play. Mother Nature didn't embed joyful play throughout the animal kingdom for no reason.

"Play Science" is an emerging discipline that is making its way into academic scholarship, onto university campuses and into the most leading-edge companies. Play Scientists now know that play covers a wide range of experiences and behaviors not only in humans, but throughout the animal kingdom. They are discovering that play is much more than simply a "fun activity."

Integrated into the human biological design, play is both highly individualized and a shared experience, and difficult to define. Like love, play is impossible to measure. And like love, play has unifying qualities.

We know play when we see it. We all light up when we watch puppies frolicking. We also know when we have played; we feel refreshed, revitalized and reinvigorated. Perhaps that is why George Bernard Shaw said, "We don't stop playing because we grow old; we grow old because we stop playing."

Play occurs in unlimited ways, and not everyone plays the same. What unifies the myriad expressions of play is an incredibly deep engagement where experienced fragmentation of our inner and outer worlds yields to the integration of unity and wholeness.

Attunement

This deep engagement is called *attunement*. If you open yourself up to it, you will discover and experience attunement all around you.

Consider an orchestra composed of many separate instruments and players. The symphony can only play coherently and creatively as one when its individual instruments and players are attuned with one another.

Attunement in humans begins in the bonding experience between mother or caregiver and child, with the early exchange of smiles and the eruption of joy and trust that follows. This model of early play, which is beneficial for both mother and child, is one that underlies all subsequent human play.

As the child continues to grow and develop, his or her unique talents begin to emerge through the exploration of self-directed play. This self-organizing play mirrors the self-organizing emergent systems scientists are discovering, from the microcosm (subatomic particles) to the macrocosm (galaxies). Perhaps the heart-wisdom of artists, poet-saints and sages has correctly intuited the universe as inherently playful!

Research and collation of thousands of play histories, from murderers to Nobel Laureates and everyone in between, has revealed that the most successful and talented people in life are those who played. Their play interests were identified and supported early in life, and their unique play talents were encouraged.

The most successful adults don't experience a separation between work and play. Their work is their play!

The joy of play begins to break down as play becomes "coerced." This happens when we feel pressured to participate in activities that are considered playful or important by others, well-meaning parents for example, and we just don't experience the fun in it. Attunement is absent.

Freedom is an inherent component in authentic play. The power and joy of play are lost when it becomes corrupted by over-control or when it becomes "scripted." Unfortunately, the joy and benefits of play can be suppressed and contorted by parents more interested in living out their own needs through their child's performance than they are in encouraging their child's natural interests. These parents don't recognize the inherent potential of their child's unique play proclivities, but rather assert their own personal agendas, such as steering their child to become the star athlete or scholar that they never became.

Something similar can occur in adult work environments with a boss or corporate culture that doesn't see the talents in their employees or recognize the potential of their unique contributions. Such work environments lack the lightness, trust and flexibility of play, with its inherent ingenuity and creativity, and hinder the ability of the employee to "come into one's own."

Play Signatures

Play Scientists now know that play has certain "signatures."

Typically, *play is voluntary*; it is done for its own sake. If the goal of the activity is more important than the involvement in the activity itself, it usually is not playful.

Play often appears purposeless. This could be why many of us in our goal-oriented culture trivialize and consider play unproductive. Play Scientists know that although play *appears* purposeless, it is anything but. Play is in fact extremely necessary not only to our health and well-being, but to our survival. It has capacities to increase perseverance and progressive mastery. Yet, paradoxically, when we play, these are not our objectives.

> ### "The opposite of play is not work, it is depression."
> —*Brian Sutton-Smith*

Play is not pressured by time constraints. When we are in deep engagement and playing, time seems to fly out the window. In fact, neuroscience research suggests play is its own "state of being," similar to sleep and dreams, and perhaps just as important.

Play is fun! We delight in the deep involvement of play and are driven to it again and again because of its inherent joyfulness and benefits. Think of the squeals of the toddler being swung around by her father: "Do it again, Daddy, do it again!"

Finally, *play takes us out of our own limited self-consciousness.* Play is how we get out of our own way and open ourselves up to the exploration of the possible. Play provides us with a creative advantage and propels innovation.

Probably the biggest contribution of contemporary Play Science research is that we now know play is anything but trivial or optional. Play is a fundamental survival drive we must honor if we value our health and well-being. Play is as important to humans as adequate nutrition or sleep.

Like other basic survival drives such as caretaking, sex and hunger, play urges come from the deep survival centers of the brain. Like sleep, we can get along without play for a period of time. And like sleep, if we have not integrated this basic survival drive into our lives, we will feel negative consequences that will impact our health, well-being and ability to thrive and cope.

Innovative Advantage

In a rapidly changing world, both creativity and innovation are needed to achieve and maintain a competitive advantage. Companies such as Google and 3M know this and allow self-organized play within the workplace.

Global economic trends are leading the way for the emergence of the "creative economy." Assembly-line industrial-age linear thinking is obsolete.

It has been said that play is the greatest natural resource in a creative economy. We are now realizing that the future favors the survival of the most nimble and resilient. So when unexpected challenges occur, play helps us respond adaptively to a new situation with more robust resources and skills.

> ### "Play is how humans learn to resolve conflict and build community."

Our global playground needs the power and joy of play to build intimacy and trust, both essential to healthy relationships.

Another way that play enhances our individual and collective lives is its crucial role in the development of empathy. The ability to put oneself in another person's shoes and feel for their experience is derived from shared playful interactions. These interactions foster the capacities for social attunement, the essence of social play. Play Science research into the lives of mass murderers and homicidal males revealed a deficiency in the ability to empathize, lack of self-regulation and a history of severe play deprivation. Combining a lack of empathy with an underdeveloped capacity to handle stress and a deficiency in resiliency—all qualities developed by play—comprises a toxic equation with devastating, often violent, real-world consequences we must begin to recognize and understand. Play is not trivial or optional.

Play is how humans learn to resolve conflict and build community. Play is the glue that holds us together while serving as the lubrication to help us through challenging times. If we lose a job or hit tough times, non-players typically respond in fear and simply "hunker down" or "dig in" hoping things go back to normal. They lack the emotional buoyancy needed for their own re-creation and personal growth.

From dogmatic religious fundamentalism and political fanaticism, to road rage and the US Congress, play is usually absent where extremism, rigidity and gridlock are found in individuals and organizations.

We now know that play is how humans develop the ability to manage their behavior. Any classroom teacher will agree that self-regulation is needed by all children to sit still, focus and learn. Those lacking in this ability are frequently impulsive and are unable to think before acting, which is typical of children labeled as having ADHD.

Yet another of play's rewards is that it prompts us to be continuously physically active, combating obesity and enhancing overall health and emotional well-being. By engaging fully in play, we can interrupt and reverse the smoldering damage of chronic stress. Play even gives the immune system a bounce!

We are built through play and built to play for a lifetime.

Reconnecting

Human beings are *neotenous,* which means we retain certain juvenile characteristics throughout the whole of our lives. We are the most playful of all animals on Earth!

Humans are presumably the most intelligent of all species. Play and intelligence are linked. Play literally feeds the brain's development of new connections and plasticity.

Unlike other animals that have adapted to specific environments, humans can inhabit all areas of the Earth, from the freezing far reaches of the Arctic to the scorching deserts of the Sahara. We spend extended time deep under the oceans and high in the stratosphere, and we can now explore the mysteries of outer space. No other animal has developed these capabilities and adaptations. Humans did not acquire such phenomenal resiliency and adaptive ability through the ages by simply sitting on a couch!

As human play has moved from its origins in natural settings to the urban parks and streets, and finally to the structured and omnipresent virtual screen play of today, some Play Scientists are concerned about what is now called "nature deficit."

Because the love of the natural world and a positive environmental ethic come from playing in nature, some Play Scientists feel that our nature deficit indicates trouble and may compromise our survival as a species. They question whether we are developing a biophobic generation, uninterested in preserving nature and her diversity.

Play is the way we become fully expressed human beings, healthy and sustainable individually and as a global community. We must play with Mother Nature, not bully, dominate and suppress her. How do we do this? Actually, it's quite simple. We just have to play more!

Critical Thinking

1. What do the authors mean by attunement and how can teachers best support this in an early childhood setting?

2. Write two paragraphs for a school newsletter on the benefits of young children engaging in play activities.

Internet References

National Institute for Play
   www.nifplay.org
The Exuberant Animal
   www.exuberantanimal.com/index.php
The Early Learning Community
   www.earlylearningcommunity.org/page/importance-of-play
Child Action, Incorporated
   www.childaction.org/families/publications/docs/guidance/Handout13-The_Importance_of_Play.pdf

---

STUART BROWN, MD, is founder and president of the National Institute for Play (*www.nifplay.org*) based in California. Dr. Brown co-teaches "From Play to Innovation" at Stanford University's d.school.

KRISTEN COZAD is the Institute's director of development and cofounder of PlayNovation, LLC. Through their work with the Institute they are dedicated to bringing the transformative power of play to public consciousness, policy and action. They also consult and present internationally on Play Science.

Brown, Stuart; Cozad, Kristen. From *SGI Quarterly*, July 2013, pp. 2–4. Copyright ©2013 by Stuart Brown and Kristen Cozad. Used with permission by the authors.

Article   Prepared by: Karen Menke Paciorek, *Eastern Michigan University*

The Importance of Equal Pay between Pre-K and K-3rd Teachers

ANNA SILLERS

Learning Outcomes

After reading this article, you will be able to:

- Advocate for compensation parity between pre-K teachers and their K-3rd grade counterparts.
- Articulate that the lack of equal compensation leads to high turnover rates among teachers, which can have a negative effect on a student's education.

According to the National Institute for Early Education Research (NIEER), more than half of all state-funded pre-K programs now require lead teachers to possess bachelor's degrees. While requiring pre-K teachers to have college degrees is intended to improve learning, it can also backfire. When teachers are required to have the same education as kindergarten teachers, but are not provided equal pay and benefits (pre-K teachers in school-sponsored settings with a bachelor's degree earn on average **80 percent** of the compensation kindergarten teachers receive), many may leave their position. This leads to higher turnover rates of pre-K teachers and an unstable workforce.

One solution is to promote compensation parity between pre-K teachers and their K-3rd grade counterparts, according to **a recent brief** and **report** from the Center for the Study of Child Care Employment (CSCCE) and NIEER. The twin publications examine the compensation policies of all 44 states that currently operate state-funded pre-K programs.

In the brief, authors make clear that compensation parity between pre-K teachers and K-3 teachers is more than just equivalent salary. They argue full compensation parity requires three things:

- Parity between salary schedules (or differentiated salaries based on qualifications and years of experience)
- Benefit parity (equivalent paid time off and health/retirement benefits), and
- parity in payment for professional responsibilities, such as time for planning and professional development.

Because very few states have explicit policies that include all these components of compensation, CSCCE and NIEER conducted detailed examinations of states that at least have salary parity policies. They found that parity policies for pre-K teachers vary widely across and within states. Fourteen states have salary parity policies in place that require the same starting salary and salary schedule as K-3 teachers.

Only four states (New Jersey, Oklahoma, Tennessee, and West Virginia) offer full compensation parity for lead pre-K teachers (participating in a state public pre-K program) in public and private settings. The effect of a lack of parity between settings can be seen in the mixed reaction to New York City Mayor Bill de Blasio's announcement last month that **the city will strive to offer universal pre-K** to all three-year-olds in addition to four-year-olds who already have access. While this comes as good news for many parents and children, **some directors of private childcare centers expressed worry** that they will lose teachers to the expanded public pre-K since New York City's education department offers higher salaries to pre-K teachers than most private centers can.

In order to achieve parity between pre-K teachers and their K-3 peers, the authors write that advocates must educate others on what compensation parity is and why it's important. Additionally, the authors suggest that stakeholders gather data on current disparities among pre-K and K-3 educators in an effort to bring attention to the gaps in compensation parity and how such gaps can undermine program quality.

Parity compensation for pre-K teachers can benefit states in ways besides reducing turnover rates. The authors found that states that report having a salary parity policy are more likely to have higher pre-K teacher wages, score higher on other **measures of NIEER's pre-K quality**, and have higher child enrollment in pre-K. But even more broadly, parity among pre-K teachers can contribute to a stable workforce, leading to higher quality care and instruction.

Critical Thinking

1. What are the ramifications of teachers being compensated differently based on the age level of children they teach?

2. How would you explain the importance of parity to parents and educators who work with elementary children?

Internet References

It doesn't pay to be an Early Childhood Teacher
http://www.npr.org/sections/ed/2016/06/14/481920837/it-doesnt-pay-to-be-an-early-childhood-teacher

Preschool Teacher Salaries
https://www.preschoolteacher.org/salaries/

Troubling pay gap for early childhood teachers
https://www.ed.gov/news/press-releases/fact-sheet-troubling-pay-gap-early-childhood-teachers

ANNA SILLERS was an intern with New America's Early and Elementary Education department.

Sillers, Anna, "The Importance of Equal Pay between Pre-K and K-3rd Teachers," *New America*, May 24, 2017.

Article   Prepared by: Karen Menke Paciorek, *Eastern Michigan University*

6 Policies to Support the Early Childhood Workforce

REBECCA ULLRICH, KATIE HAMM, AND LEILA SCHOCHET

Learning Outcomes

After reading this article, you will be able to:

- Articulate the benefits for young children of paying teachers a livable and equitable wage in relation to their job performance and responsibilities.

- Explain to others how staffing and ratios affect the discrepancy between the high cost of childcare and low teachers' wages.

- List steps that could be taken to maintain a professional development system in this country.

Introduction and Summary

America's economy is dependent in no small measure on the 2 million educators who comprise the early childhood workforce.[1] Without this largely female workforce, millions of working parents with no or few high-quality childcare options would be unable to participate in the U.S. labor force. Despite the importance of early childhood educators—to the economy, parents, and young children—low wages, minimal benefits, and a lack of professional supports are commonplace.

One of those early educators is Carmella Salinas, who was interviewed by *The New York Times* in July 2016.[2] According to *The New York Times*, Salinas earns just $12.89 per hour as a teacher in a childcare center in Española, New Mexico, after almost 15 years in the field. Her center cannot afford to provide her with benefits, so she is limited to working 32 hr per week. This past summer, however, Salinas was without work because not enough parents could afford the center's full tuition, which is offset by pre-K funds during the school year. Salinas had to wait for a new school year to begin in September when state pre-K funds could pay her salary.

The volatility of her wage situation has taken a toll on Salinas and her family. She struggles to afford her utility bills, and it takes her months to save enough money to cover additional expenses such as car repairs. At one point, Salinas got a second job to supplement her childcare wages. She then earned too much to qualify for Medicaid and the Supplemental Nutrition Assistance Program but too little to comfortably afford groceries and the two inhalers she needs for her chronic asthma. Salinas told *The New York Times* that she found herself rationing the medication—taking just one puff instead of four per day—to save money.

The story from *The New York Times* went on to explain that many early educators—including Salinas—have limited opportunities for career advancement. Although policy makers and researchers increasingly see a bachelor's degree as a needed credential for high-quality care programs, degree programs are inaccessible to many teachers. While New Mexico, for example, offers a stipend to help teachers earn degrees and stay in the field, underfunding means that the program nevertheless falls far short of covering the cost of attending and graduating from college for many teachers. Salinas' stipend only covers one class per semester, but there is simply no way she can afford the cost of extra classes on top of meeting basic needs.[3] Consequently, she has been taking classes toward her bachelor's degree for more than a decade.

Salinas' experience is not unique: Early educators across the country struggle to make ends meet on dismal wages and limited benefits. Childcare workers and preschool teachers are in the bottom quintile of annual salaries in the United States, averaging less than $30,000 per year.[4] Childcare workers are

Targeted supports for working student teachers—such as scholarship programs, evening or online classes, and coursework offered in multiple languages—can help maintain diversity and reduce stratification across roles.[45]

Policies to Support a Professional Early Childhood Workforce

Significant advancements in early care and education policy are long overdue. It is critical that the United States shifts away from piecemeal initiatives toward comprehensive reform. Future legislation must infuse enough funding to simultaneously reduce costs for low- and middle-income families, promote high-quality services, and improve conditions for the workforce. The Center for American Progress proposed one possible approach that would expand tax credits for childcare and funding for voluntary universal preschool—calibrated to the cost of operating full-day, high-quality programs.[46] These strategies would provide programs with higher levels of funding per child, which would serve to boost early educator salaries.

On top of a new financing approach, reform must address the existing barriers and challenges created by historical underfunding and fragmentation. Solutions aimed at only addressing one problem—such as increasing education and training requirements without improving compensation—will likely exacerbate the existing problems with turnover and have a disproportionate impact on teachers from lower-income communities and the children they serve.

The following six policies should be incorporated into federal reform for early childhood care and education with the goal of promoting a professional early childhood workforce. These policies should ultimately be implemented by states in partnership with the federal government.

Develop and Maintain a Comprehensive Professional Development System

States need coordinated professional development systems to prepare and train a skilled early childhood workforce. The benefits of professional development are maximized through a coordinated network of education, training, and technical assistance.[47] Various forms of professional development should both align with and inform one another such that they work in combination to provide teachers with core knowledge and skills.

Federal legislation must include a stable federal investment that, in combination with state dollars, funds the development and maintenance of comprehensive professional development systems. These systems should be available to teachers across programs, settings, and roles. States should work with stakeholders—including institutes of higher education, vocational or technical schools, professional development providers, and other credentialing bodies—to design a system of professional development opportunities that meets the following criteria:

- **Has credentials with labor market value:** Credentials have labor market value when they qualify early educators to fulfill a particular role or position.[48] More advanced credentials should allow teachers to progress forward on a given state's early childhood career pathway, leading to more advanced roles and higher compensation.[49]

- **Has portable credentials:** Credentials should be portable or widely accepted as a verification of teacher qualifications.[50] This means credentials are acknowledged across educational institutions; program settings; and ultimately, across states. A teacher with a particular credential should be qualified to fulfill a corresponding role in a childcare center, Head Start, or state pre-K classroom.[51]

- **Has stackable credentials:** Stackable credentials build upon each other, are reflective of increasing knowledge and skill, and typically connect progressive levels of education.[52] Stackable credentials can help early educators make the jump from shorter-term certificate programs to longer-term degree programs.

- **Is accessible:** Education and training must be targeted to early educators balancing coursework with full- or part-time employment. Programs should be available through a mixture of online and in-person mediums, during the evenings and weekends, and in accessible locations. Coursework and training must also be available in multiple languages to support non-native speakers.

- **Extends beyond traditional coursework:** Teachers should have the opportunity to participate in shorter-term workshops and trainings that target specific knowledge or skills and complement classroom-based learning.

- For example, a teacher might participate in a series of workshops related to integrating technology into the classroom or effective data collection practices. Trainings and workshops should be augmented by supervised practice in the classroom. In particular, states should establish forms of continuous technical assistance such as mentoring and coaching to support ongoing skill development.

- **Provides credit for prior learning:** Early educators should have opportunities to demonstrate what they know and are able to do and apply those acquired skills toward credential attainment. Receiving credit for prior learning allows early educators to focus on new or lesser-developed content and competencies at their own pace.

- **Includes measures for quality assurance:** States should articulate the required credentials for professional development providers—including individual trainers, mentors, coaches, and consultants—as well as sponsoring organizations. Moreover, states must engage in continuous monitoring and evaluation to ensure that professional development is reflective of the most recent research and standards of practice.[53]

Develop or Revise Statewide Career Pathways

The U.S. Department of Health and Human Services identified career pathways as a key strategy to help states and programs address inconsistent compensation, expectations, and professional development across sectors.[54] Career pathways identify a sequence of credentials that are reflective of progressively higher competencies and are tied to particular roles or job titles. When used across early childhood programs, career pathways can reduce fragmentation in program standards for staff and provide a clear road map for early childhood professionals to advance.

While most states have done some work to sequence early childhood credentials, career pathways are often not meaningfully implemented in early childhood programs.[55] For instance, such approaches are not used consistently in early childhood programs across the state, nor are they necessarily tied to advancing roles and compensation in the workplace. Most state ladders or pathways are only used in select programs or are used solely to inform individual teachers' professional development. These limitations inhibit the ability of any given state's efforts to advance early care and education as a profession.

Federal legislation should support states in developing robust career pathways that accomplish the following goals:

- Provide a shared understanding of expectations for teachers' knowledge base, skills, and credentials to create consistent standards across the early childhood education field. Education and skills should be tied to a job title that is uniform across early childhood settings.[56]
- Offer a progression for career development that individuals can use to set career goals and identify steps to meet those goals. This approach allows for specialization based on job characteristics such as age group or function and also provides clear guidance for advancement.

- Establish compensation standards based on education or training.
- Provide opportunities for advancement and increased specialization. Pathways should articulate the skills and competencies required to be promoted to a new position or to remain in the same role but move to a new program or serve a different age group of children. As staff advance, the pathway should also reflect opportunities for increasingly specific tracks or specialties, such as program management and business administration, coordination of educational programming, or early childhood special education.[57]
- Guide other early childhood systems. For example, professional development systems should all be reflective of the competencies and credentials outlined in the career pathway.[58] Likewise, a state's quality rating and improvement system, or QRIS, should use the career pathway to define progressively higher teacher requirements to advance to higher-quality ratings.

Make Progress toward Compensation and Benefit Standards at Parity with Kindergarten Teachers

Including compensation and benefits as formal indicators of quality clearly communicates that teachers' economic well-being is part of quality in all settings and that a program cannot be of high quality if teachers are not earning a living wage. Federal legislation should require that states add compensation and benefit standards to their QRIS.[59] Specifically, standards should require:

- Tiered salary schedules at each level of quality, such that early childhood educators at all levels earn increasingly higher salaries as program quality increases.
- At the base level of quality, entry-level professionals to earn a living wage and have access to a comprehensive benefits package.
- At the highest levels of quality,[60] lead teachers or equivalent positions to earn salary parity with kindergarten teachers in the local school district.
- Any staff member working at least the equivalent of a full school day and year to be salaried rather than paid on an hourly basis.

The federal government should also lead by example and create wage parity for Head Start teachers in the next reauthorization. Although ¾ of Head Start teachers now have a bachelor's degree, they earn $31,242 annually—more than $20,000 less than the average kindergarten teacher salary.[61] Likewise, the federal government should leverage Preschool Development Grants and any subsequent federal preschool funding to encourage states to address compensation disparities within their public pre-K programs. As described in previous sections, existing parity policies fall short of serving many teachers in the public pre-K system. Teachers in public pre-K classrooms—both in public schools as well as in community-based settings—should earn salaries and benefits on par with kindergarten teachers in the local public school district.

While family childcare providers can be seamlessly integrated into many policy solutions—including credential requirements and professional development supports—addressing compensation for the home-based workforce is complex. As small-business owners, family childcare providers have some agency around the number of children they care for and the number of hours they work, which affects their revenue. Increasing per-child funding levels will help increase providers' take-home pay. However, states must also develop strategies to ensure that family childcare providers who choose to work full time can earn a living wage.

Promote Data-driven Policies and Programs with a Statewide Workforce Registry

States should increase participation in their early childhood workforce registries to gather relevant information about the early childhood workforce. Early childhood workforce registries are online systems that include characteristics of early childhood workers and their programs of employment.[62] Workforce registries allow teachers to track their progress toward their professional goals, enable centers to verify teacher participation in various professional development and training opportunities, and inform state early care and education administrators about the workforce.

When the data collected in registries are robust and comprehensive, they can inform state policies around teacher credential requirements and participation in professional development, identify geographic areas in need of workers with specialized education and training, and help states target financial and technical assistance resources to underserved areas. Workforce registry data can be linked to states' QRIS to easily verify that programs have met particular standards. They can also be linked with child-level data systems to analyze associations between programs, teachers, and children for the purposes of research that improves systems and practices in the classroom.

Forty-two states have a workforce registry in place.[63] However, because most state registries are voluntary for teachers, they fall short in providing a complete picture of the status of the workforce. This ultimately limits their utility in informing policy-making and program administration.[64]

Federal legislation should require states to amend existing registries or develop new comprehensive workforce registries that:

- Collect data on teacher demographics, role or position title, compensation and benefits, degree progress and attainment, and participation in professional development.[65]
- Are linked to statewide career pathways, early childhood data systems, QRIS, and state-sponsored professional development and training courses.
- Can generate reports to inform policy planning and implementation.

Bolster State Scholarship Programs

As early childhood programs increasingly require or encourage higher credentials for staff, states must bolster their existing scholarship programs to help offset the cost of tuition and other expenses.

There are few data on scholarship recipients, but evidence suggests that these programs are fairly limited in scope and impact.[66] Scholarship awards are likely too small in amount to offset a significant amount of the cost of tuition or fees. Programs generally lack the resources to support all eligible members of the workforce in any given state.

State scholarship administrators should use data collected through their workforce registries to target scholarship funds based on the unique needs of programs and workers in their states. For example, in states where public pre-K teachers are required to have a bachelor's degree, policy makers may choose to target scholarship funds to teachers serving children ages 3 and younger. Other states may choose to target teachers seeking education and training in high-need specialty areas, such as early childhood special education, early intervention, or dual language learners. States should also consider prioritizing educators who may experience more significant barriers to higher education, such as teachers in rural or high-poverty communities.

Reward Degree Attainment with Wage Supplements or Tax Credits

To incentivize professional growth and retention, some states have turned to wage supplement initiatives, which provide a lump sum to teachers once or twice annually. However, wage supplements cannot replace an increase in compensation across the board for the early childhood workforce, nor do onetime bonuses truly offset the upfront costs of higher education and training. Instead, states should consider the following strategies as a means of providing bonuses or incentives to early childhood educators.

The Child Care WAGE$ Project is an example of a wage supplement program for early educators. WAGE$ is administered by nonprofit organizations in Florida, Iowa, Kansas, New Mexico, and North Carolina.[67] Teachers, directors, and family childcare providers earning below an hourly wage threshold are eligible for a twice-yearly supplement based on their highest level of education. The average six-month supplement is $952.[68] In 2015, nearly 6,000 members of the early childhood workforce received wage supplements through WAGE$. The WAGE$ program is typically funded through a mixture of private and public sources, depending on the state.[69]

State-funded tax credits for members of the early childhood workforce are an emerging strategy to promote and reward continuing education, training, and retention.[70] At present, Louisiana and Nebraska have adopted a tax credit program for the early childhood workforce. While eligibility for participating teachers varies, both states award higher tax credits to teachers with higher levels of education and credentials. In some states, tax credits are a preferable funding mechanism—compared with other wage supplements—because, as part of the tax system, they are stable and not subject to approval each year.

The federal government should provide flexible resources to states that choose to adopt some form of ongoing, stable bonus or incentive structure to promote continuing education and advancement within the field of early childhood education.

Conclusion

The early care and education system is at a crossroads. The need for working parents to access early care and education is critical and well-documented, as is the need for that care to be of high quality in order to realize long-term positive benefits for children's learning and development. In order to dramatically improve early childhood program quality, the federal government must support states in building and maintaining a professional early childhood workforce: one with uniform standards for preparation and training; a clearly defined pathway for career advancement; fair compensation and comprehensive benefits; and robust supports for continuing education and training. By adopting these policies as part of systemic reform, conditions will improve not only for the early childhood workforce but also for the millions of children and families who rely on early educators every day.

Acknowledgments

The authors thank our colleagues at the Center for American Progress for their review of previous drafts of this report: David A. Bergeron, Ben Miller, Angela Hanks, Karla Walter, Rachel Herzfeldt-Kamprath, Jessica Troe, and Simon Workman. We also extend our appreciation to Meg Benner, Jaya Chatterjee, Netsy Firestein, Lauren Hogan, Kat Kempe, Lea J.E. Austin, and Marcy Whitebook for their helpful insight.

Finally, the authors would like to acknowledge Mary Jo Smith and Jenna Conway of the Louisiana Department of Education for their help in verifying information in this report.

Notes

1. National Survey of Early Care and Education Project Team, "Number and Characteristics of Early Care and Education (ECE) Teachers and Caregivers: Initial Findings from the National Survey of Early Care and Education (NSECE)" (2013), available at http://www.acf.hhs.gov/sites/default/files/opre/nsece_wf_brief_102913_0.pdf.

2. Patricia Cohen, "Child Care Expansion Takes a Toll on Poorly Paid Workers," *The New York Times*, July 12, 2016, available at http://www.nytimes.com/2016/07/13/business/economy/child-care-expansion-takes-a-toll-on-poorly-paid-workers.html?_r=0.

3. Ibid.

4. Bureau of Labor Statistics, "Occupational Employment and Wages, May 2015: 39-9011 Childcare Workers," available at http://www.bls.gov/oes/current/oes399011.htm (last accessed November 2016); Bureau of Labor Statistics, "Occupational Employment and Wages, May 2015: 25-2011 Preschool Teachers, Except Special Education," available at http://www.bls.gov/oes/current/oes252011.htm (last accessed November 2016).

5. Elise Gould, "Child care workers aren't paid enough to make ends meet" (Washington: Economic Policy Institute, 2015), available at http://www.epi.org/publication/child-care-workers-arent-paid-enough-to-make-ends-meet/.

6. Lynda Laughlin, "Who's Minding the Kids? Child Care Arrangements: Spring 2011" (Washington: Bureau of the Census, 2013), available at https://www.census.gov/prod/2013pubs/p70-135.pdf.

7. National Survey of Early Care and Education Project Team, "Number and Characteristics of Early Care and Education (ECE) Teachers and Caregivers."

8. Office of Child Care, "FY 2014 Preliminary Data Table 15—Average Monthly Subsidy Paid to Provider by Age Group and Care Type," August 13, 2015, available at http://www.acf.hhs.gov/occ/resource/fy-2014-preliminary-data-table-15.

9. Child Care Aware of America, "Parents and the High Cost of Child Care: 2015 Report" (2015), available at http://usa.childcareaware.org/wp-content/uploads/2016/03/Parents-and-the-High-Cost-of-Child-Care-2015-FINAL.pdf.

Article   Prepared by: Karen Menke Paciorek, *Eastern Michigan University*

The Hell of American Day Care

An Investigation into the Barely Regulated, Unsafe Business of Looking After Our Children

JONATHAN COHN

Learning Outcomes

After reading this article, you will be able to:

- Describe the economic importance of all children attending high-quality child care.

- Name three reasons why regulations for child care providers are so difficult to enforce.

- Share with parents points they should consider when looking for child care.

Trusting your child with someone else is one of the hardest things that a parent has to do—and in the United States, it's harder still, because American day care is a mess. About 8.2 million kids—about 40 percent of children under five—spend at least part of their week in the care of somebody other than a parent. Most of them are in centers, although a sizable minority attend home day cares. . . . In other countries, such services are subsidized and well-regulated. In the United States, despite the fact that work and family life has changed profoundly in recent decades, we lack anything resembling an actual child care system. Excellent day cares are available, of course, if you have the money to pay for them and the luck to secure a spot. But the overall quality is wildly uneven and barely monitored, and at the lower end, it's Dickensian.

This situation is especially disturbing because, over the past two decades, researchers have developed an entirely new understanding of the first few years of life. This period affects the architecture of a child's brain in ways that indelibly shape intellectual abilities and behavior. Kids who grow up in nurturing, interactive environments tend to develop the skills they need to thrive as adults—like learning how to calm down after a setback or how to focus on a problem long enough to solve it. Kids who grow up without that kind of attention tend to lack impulse control and have more emotional outbursts. Later on, they are more likely to struggle in school or with the law. They also have more physical health problems. Numerous studies show that all children, especially those from low-income homes, benefit greatly from sound child care. The key ingredients are quite simple—starting with plenty of caregivers, who ideally have some expertise in child development.

By these metrics, American day care performs abysmally. A 2007 survey by the National Institute of Child Health Development deemed the majority of operations to be "fair" or "poor"—only 10 percent provided high-quality care. Experts recommend a ratio of one caregiver for every three infants between six and 18 months, but just one-third of children are in settings that meet that standard. Depending on the state, some providers may need only minimal or no training in safety, health, or child development. And because child care is so poorly paid, it doesn't attract the highly skilled. In 2011, the median annual salary for a child care worker was $19,430, less than a parking lot attendant or a janitor. Marcy Whitebook, the director of the Center for the Study of Child Care Employment at the University of California-Berkeley, told me, "We've got decades of research, and it suggests most child care and early childhood education in this country is mediocre at best."

At the same time, day care is a bruising financial burden for many families—more expensive than rent in 22 states. In the priciest, Massachusetts, it costs an average family $15,000 a year to place an infant full-time in a licensed center. In California, the cost is equivalent to 40 percent of the median income for a single mother.

Only minimal assistance is available to offset these expenses. The very poorest families receive a tax credit worth up to $1,050 a year per child. Some low-income families can also get subsidies or vouchers, but in most states the waiting lists for them are long. And so many parents put their kids in whatever they can find and whatever they can afford, hoping it will be good enough.

One indicator of the importance that the United States places on child care is how little official information the country bothers to collect about it. There are no regular surveys of quality and no national database of safety problems. One of the only serious studies, by Julia Wrigley and Joanna Dreby, appeared in the *American Sociological Review* in 2005. The researchers cobbled together a database of fatalities from state records, court documents, and media reports. On the surface, they said, day care appears "quite safe," but looking closer, they discovered "striking differences." The death rate for infants in home settings—whether in their own houses with a nanny or in home day cares—was seven times higher than in centers. The most common causes included drowning, violence—typically, caregivers shaking babies—and fire.

Statistics on Sudden Infant Death Syndrome (SIDS) are also revealing. ChildCare Aware of America, an advocacy group, calculated that, proportionally, about 9 percent of all reported SIDS deaths should take place in child care. The actual number is twice that. And while overall SIDS fatalities declined after a nationwide education campaign, the death rate in child care held steady.

Fatalities in child care remain relatively rare, but not as rare as they should be. In an investigation of Missouri day cares, *St. Louis Post-Dispatch* reporter Nancy Cambria documented 45 deaths between 2007 and 2010. One was three-month-old William Pratt, who died from blunt trauma after a caregiver threw him on a couch because she was frustrated with him. In 2012, a toddler named Juan Carlos Cardenas wandered off at an Indiana church day care. Nobody was watching him when he fell, face-first, into a baptismal pool and drowned.

Kenya Mire was an only child and hated it, and perhaps that's why she liked kids so much. After finishing high school, in 1999, she started training to be a medical assistant, hoping to work in a maternity ward. "I was just so interested in the idea of pregnancy," she says in her clear, measured way. "I always wanted to be that person where I was in the room with them from the time when they came in up through when they had the baby. I wanted to be the person that you told your story to."

When she was 22, however, Mire had to put her plans on hold, because she was pregnant herself. She and the father weren't together and her morning sickness got so bad she had to quit her job in a restaurant kitchen and move in with her mom. Despite all that, she felt "worry-free," she says. "I was just so excited to have a child." Eight years later, when she got pregnant again, it was different. This time, she knew how hard it would be.

When Mire went back to work, she put Kendyll in the same day care where she'd sent her son, Bryce: Grandma's Place—a bright, cheery operation with a professional staff. But Grandma's Place was expensive. Even with the subsidies Texas provides to low-income mothers, Mire had to pay $200 a week from her $12.50-an-hour job at a water utility company. Then the recession hit, and Mire lost the job. She had to pull Kendyll from the center.

Mire's dilemma was one that American parents, particularly single mothers, have struggled with for generations. The United States has always been profoundly uncomfortable with the idea of supporting child care outside the home, for reasons that inevitably trace back to beliefs over the proper role of women and mothers. At no point has a well-organized public day care system ever been considered the social ideal.

The first day cares were established during the Industrial Revolution, as increasing numbers of women in cities had to work. Jane Addams, the Progressive Era activist, was horrified to learn that all over Chicago, children were being left alone in tenement homes, morning till night. "The first three crippled children we encountered in the neighborhood had all been injured while their mothers were at work," she wrote in her 1910 memoir, *Twenty Years at Hull-House*. "One had fallen out of a third-story window, another had been burned, and the third had a curved spine due to the fact that for three years he had been tied all day long to the leg of the kitchen table, only released at noon by his older brother who hastily ran in from a neighboring factory to share his lunch with him."

Addams and other do-gooders created "day nurseries," although in many cities they were little more than baby farms. Geraldine Youcha writes in *Minding the Children* that a survey from that era by Chicago authorities "found children unclean and crowded into one small room without any playthings, and several nurseries in which the 'superintendent' did not even know the last names and addresses of some of the children."

The prevailing assumption at the time was that child care outside the home was deeply inferior to a mother's care. At best, it was regarded as a useful tool to "Americanize" the children of recent immigrants. Even Addams believed the optimal solution was government subsidies that would allow single mothers to look after their own children. ("With all of the efforts made by modern society to nurture and educate the young, how stupid it is to permit the mothers of young children to spend themselves in the coarser work of the world!" she wrote.) Toward that end, progressive states created widows' pensions, which were eventually expanded by the New Deal. Decades later, most people would know this kind of assistance simply as "welfare."

Arguably the best child care system America has ever had emerged during World War II, when women stepped in to fill the jobs of absent soldiers. For the first time, women were employed outside the home in a manner that society approved of, or at least tolerated. But many of these women had nowhere to leave their small children. They resorted to desperate measures—locking kids in the car in the factory parking lot, with the windows cracked open and blankets stretched across the back seats. This created the only moment in American politics when child care was ever a national priority. In 1940, Congress passed the Lanham Act, which created a system of government-run centers that served more than 100,000 children from families of all incomes.

After the war, children's advocates wanted to keep the centers open. But lawmakers saw them only as a wartime contingency—and if day care enabled women to keep their factory jobs, veterans would have a harder time finding work. The Lanham Act was allowed to lapse.

The federal government didn't get back into the child care business until the 1960s, with the creation of Head Start, which was narrowly targeted to support low-income children. A broader bill, designed to help working mothers by providing care to all kids who needed it, passed Congress a few years later. But President Nixon vetoed the legislation, saying he didn't want the government getting mixed up with "communal" child-rearing arrangements. Other than some increases in government funding for child tax credits and subsidies, federal child care policy has hardly changed in the last few decades.

But family life has changed immeasurably. In 1975, most American families had a male breadwinner and a female homemaker, compared with one in five today. Around two-thirds of mothers of young children now work outside the home.

Meanwhile, the idea that it is preferable to support low-income women to stay home with their children has become toxic in American politics. Since the passage of welfare reform in 1996, single mothers no longer get cash benefits unless they have a job or demonstrate progress toward getting one. Millions of women with meager resources who would have qualified under the old welfare regime must find somewhere for their young children to go while they're at work.

Day care, in other words, has become a permanent reality, although the public conversation barely reflects that fact. The issue of child care is either neglected as a "women's issue" or obsessed over in mommy-wars debates about the virtues of day care versus stay-at-home moms. Whether out of reluctance to acknowledge a fundamental change in the conception of parenthood—especially motherhood—or out of a fear of expanding the role of government in family life, we still haven't come to terms with the shift of women from the home to the workplace.

In many countries, day care is treated not as an afterthought, but as a priority. France, for instance, has a government-run system that experts consider exemplary. Infants and toddlers can attend *crèche*, which is part of the public health system, while preschoolers go to the *école maternelle,* which is part of the public education system. At every *crèche,* half the caregivers must have specialized collegiate degrees in child care or psychology; pediatricians and psychologists are available for consultation. Teachers in the *école maternelle* must have special post-college training and are paid the same as public school teachers. Neither program is mandatory, but nearly every preschooler goes to the *école maternelle.* Parents who stay at home to care for their children or hire their own caregivers receive generous tax breaks. It hardly seems a coincidence that 80 percent of French women work, compared with 60 percent of their American counterparts.

France spends more on care per child than the United States—a lot more, in the case of infants and toddlers. But most French families pay far less out of pocket, because the government subsidizes child care with tax dollars and sets fees according to a sliding scale based on income. Overall, the government devotes about 1 percent of France's gross domestic product to child care, more than twice as much as the United States does. As Steven Greenhouse once observed in *The New York Times,* "Comparing the French system with the American system . . . is like comparing a vintage bottle of Chateau Margaux with a $4 bottle of American wine."

There is one place in the United States where you can find a very similar arrangement: the military. In the 1980s, the Defense Department decided to address, rather than ignore, the same social changes that have transformed the wider economy. More women were entering the military, and many had children. Increasingly, the wives of male soldiers had jobs of their own. Believing that subsidized day care was essential for recruitment and morale, military leaders created a system the National Women's Law Center has called a "model for the nation." More than 98 percent of military child care centers meet standards set by the National Association for the Education of Young Children, compared with only 10 percent of private-sector day cares.

A growing number of economists have become convinced that a comprehensive child care system is not only a worthwhile investment, but also an essential one. James Heckman, the Nobel-winning economist, has calculated that, in the best early childhood programs, every dollar that society invests yields between $7 and $12 in benefits. When children grow up to become productive members of the workforce, they feed more money into the economy and pay more taxes. They also cost the state less—for trips to the E.R., special education, incarceration, unemployment benefits, and other expenses that have been linked to inadequate nurturing in the earliest years of life. Two Fed economists concluded in a report that "the most efficient means to boost the productivity of the workforce 15 to 20 years down the road is to invest in today's youngest children" and that such spending would yield "a much higher return than most government-funded economic development initiatives."

In a July 2012 speech, Fed Chairman Ben Bernanke made the case that significant investment in early childhood would deliver even broader gains to the U.S. economy. "Notably, a portion of these economic returns accrues to the children themselves and their families," he said, "but studies show that the rest of society enjoys the majority of the benefits." Right now, too many Americans make major choices about work or finances based on the scarcity or cost of child care. Sometimes, this means women curtail their careers because it's cheaper to stay home or take a more flexible job than to pay for full-time care. Sometimes, a person of limited means pours a significant portion of their income into day care, which limits their ability to build a financial foundation for the future. When parents can find safe, affordable child care, they are more likely to realize their full economic potential. Their employers gain, too: Numerous studies show that access to quality day care increases productivity significantly.

This year, President Barack Obama has put forward what he calls a "universal pre-kindergarten" proposal. It would provide states with matching funds, so that they could set up their own programs for three- and four-year-olds, while modestly increasing subsidies for infant and toddler care. This plan would cost $75 billion over ten years, financed by higher cigarette taxes, which means it will meet serious political resistance. But the concept has support from key Democrats like House Minority Leader Nancy Pelosi, who has spoken of "doing for child care what we did for health care."

Since the 1930s, with the introduction of Social Security, the United States has constructed—slowly, haphazardly, often painfully—a welfare state. Pensions, public housing, health care—piece by piece, the government created protections for citizens that the market doesn't always provide. Child care is the major unfinished part of that project. The lack of quality, affordable day care is arguably the most significant barrier to full equality for women in the workplace. It makes it more likely that children born in poverty will remain there. That's why other developed countries made child care a collective responsibility long ago.

Critical Thinking

1. Ask three parents using child care how they chose that particular program for their child? What is most important for them to consider and why?

2. What are the challenges parents face when looking for child care?

3. Find the average cost for a week of child care for a three-year-old in your area.

Internet References

Child Care Directory: Care Guide
www.care.com

Child Welfare League of America (CWLA)
www.cwla.org

Children's Defense Fund (CDF)
www.childrensdefense.org

Early Childhood Care and Development
www.ecdgroup.com

National Network for Child Care
www.nncc.org

National Resource Center for Health and Safety in Child Care and Early Education
http://nrckids.org

Unit 2

UNIT

Prepared by: Karen Menke Paciorek, *Eastern Michigan University*

Supporting the Development of Young Children and Their Families

Many different issues are addressed in this Unit titled: Supporting Young Children and Their Families and I invite you to reflect on your family, the types of experiences children today have as compared to you, and the ways educators can help families as they navigate the ever changing, fast-paced world while raising children. The role of fathers in the lives of their children has received renewed attention as parents work to find the many ways in which they can foster the development of their children. Mothers have traditionally taken on a significant role in rearing children but dads are increasingly taking on the responsibility of finding childcare and taking children for medical appointments. Children, like my grandson, who have a caring and invested father in their lives are so fortunate. As early childhood educators it is important for us to support families so young children can grow up in families with parents able to provide what is best for their child to thrive.

"James L. Hymes, who served as manager of the Kaiser Child Service Centers in Oregon during WWII, stated in 1970 at a conference on industry and day care, 'We did it all at a tremendous expense.' He went on to say, 'I have to end by saying this was wartime. This was a cost-plus contract . . . I am taken with how costly good services to children and families have to be. I am taken with how costly bad services always are.'" (Paciorek, 2008 p. xvi)

Hymes was referring to the high cost to society as a whole when working families do not receive the support they need to do their jobs and raise their children. He recognized that to get the ships needed for the war effort built on time childcare had to be available for the working mothers as the majority of the fathers were serving in the military. Childcare costs were a part of the total expense in building the ships. Providing support for families by sharing with them available community resources is also a part of the job of an early childhood educator. Today there are limited childcare options for children whose parents work evenings, weekends, or shifts often found in public safety and medical fields. We must do better to help these families find quality consistent care for their children.

When examining the partnerships between young children, their families, the educational setting, and the communities in which they live, one word keeps coming up again and again: relationships. The term reciprocal relationships certainly defines the two-way street that must be in operation as we all work to support the growth and learning of young children. You will see the word relationships in many of the articles along with the words supporting, connecting, and partnerships. The level of collaboration that must exist between everyone vested in the education of a child is similar to a well-choreographed dance or athletic play. Everyone has to be focused on the needs of others to effectively do their job to support the development of the young child. The chance to interact with families diminishes as the learner gets older until it is almost nonexistent at the secondary level. Early childhood educators who recognize and fully embrace the rich contributions families can make as partners in the education process will benefit and so will the children. Sharing between the parents and teachers about the strengths, needs, and interests of the child becomes the path to student success.

Increased interest in fostering healthy social and emotional development has recently been a key topic of focus in K-12 education. Many early childhood educators would say, "Well it took you long enough to get here." Meaning ECE educators have been addressing young children's development and needs in the social and emotional/affective domains for centuries. We fully recognize that a child who does not have confidence in his or her learning capabilities or feel supported and encouraged by others in their world finds it difficult to move ahead in learning new skills. Help your colleagues who may not have educational preparation focusing on a child's social and emotional developmental needs to fully integrate appropriate learning experiences into the learning setting. Share what effective ECE educators have known all along that children feeling competent as learners and supported in their explorations is critical. Provide examples of encouragement for children such as, "You two cooperated to finish that project." as opposed to saying, "Good job." Model appropriate recognition and encouragement of the work children are doing for others and demonstrate altruistic behaviors and pro-social teaching in your classroom. Use the words caring, compassion, helping, cooperation, sustainability, collaboration, empathy, along with other pro-social terms, throughout the day as you interact with young children in their learning.

Early childhood educators who are effective in providing appropriate learning experiences which foster the following four categories of learning are critical. During the early childhood years children acquire competency in content knowledge, specific skills, handling feelings in socially acceptable ways, and dispositions which will serve them for a lifetime of learning. Families can provide a wealth of information about their child, and teachers who develop strong relationships with families are beneficiaries of this knowledge. Upon doing a check of the website for a local school district I came across a principal's page at one school. There the principal posted pictures of herself as an elementary student and shared some of her likes and skills when she was younger. Children and families form connections with those who take the time to get to know them. Share a bit about yourself and your interests, and you may be rewarded with information from families about the children in your class. Build on this information to provide learning experiences that are relevant and meaningful to your children.

Teaching children the early childhood years certainly involves much more than teaching academic content. The development of the whole child must be thoughtfully addressed through the activities available for each child. Anecdotal reports from teachers of young children point to increasing aggressive behaviors displayed in classrooms with children as young as two years of age. Kicking, hitting, biting, yelling, and a whole host of other aggressive behaviors that are dangerous, destructive to materials, or disturbing the learning environment are occurring with increasing frequency. Teachers can help children displaying these behaviors by implementing a focused and consistent approach to guiding behavior. Again, the word relationships plays a key role in helping seriously disruptive children learn to be a socially acceptable member of the classroom, their family, and society. I see helping young children acquire appropriate behavioral control as the most challenging part of teaching. There are many concrete strategies for meeting standards, planning learning experiences, and assessing young children; however, addressing individual needs that impact a child's behavior requires an intentional and very individualized approach. Beginning teachers can learn from more seasoned teachers who can share strategies that have proved successful in the past.

The title of this unit, once again, must be stressed: Supporting the Development of Young Children and Their Families. Teachers who see their job of working with young children as finding the approach that best supports each child's individual development will be most successful. We are not to change children to meet some idealistic model, but become an investigator whose job is to ferret out the individual strengths and learning styles of each child in our care. Enjoy each day and the many different experiences awaiting you when you work with young children and their families.

Article   Prepared by: Karen Menke Paciorek, *Eastern Michigan University*

Making the Right Choice Simple

Selecting Materials for Infants and Toddlers

ANI N. SHABAZIAN AND CAROLINE LI SOGA

Learning Outcomes

After reading this article, you will be able to:

- Share with teachers and children's families the importance of choosing appropriate materials for infants and toddlers.

- List the criteria for safe toys.

- Describe what constitutes a developmentally appropriate material.

> It is always the children who give shape to things and not the things that shape the children. The various materials are seen in terms of their many different possibilities and transformations.
>
> —Mirella Ruozzi

As the opening quotation illustrates, infants and toddlers are not passive recipients of the world around them but rather are active participants continuously engaging with their environment. Thus, young children need a world that is safe to explore, one where they are encouraged to venture and discover. An infant's world should be replete with opportunities to see, hear, feel, touch, taste, smell, and move. This article explores ways to optimize the various possibilities and transformations materials provide for infants and toddlers (Ruozzi 2010). For our purposes we define *materials* as objects that children interact with, and we particularly value those that encourage physical exploration. We address two questions: (1) What criteria should teachers use to select infant and toddler materials? (2) How should materials look, feel, and sound?

Criteria for Selecting Play Materials

A thoughtful, intentional selection of materials ensures a dynamic and evolving environment that promotes learning. The following considerations apply when choosing materials for infants (birth to 18 months) and toddlers (18 months to 3 years): Are the materials developmentally appropriate and do they encourage active participation? Are they open-ended, healthy and safe, and neutral and nonbiased?

Developmentally Appropriate Materials

NAEYC states that developmentally appropriate practices take into account what is known about the individual child, what is known about child development and learning, and what is known about the child's culture (NAEYC 2009a). First, in selecting developmentally appropriate materials, it is important to use knowledge about children's individual interests and approaches to learning. This helps ensure that teachers meet and cultivate children's interests and needs. For example, asking 14-month-old Clara to throw a ball forward into a basket five feet away is outside of Clara's zone of proximal development—what she knows and is able to do. This sets her up for failure and may negatively impact her sense of self-competence. However, Clara enjoys sorting balls into different-size containers. To recognize their own abilities and build their social-emotional development, infants and toddlers need to feel a sense of competence and satisfaction with the materials they engage with on a regular basis (Copple & Bredekamp 2009).

Second, teachers can use their knowledge about children's development to make general predictions about a particular age group and their capabilities and provide materials appropriate for the children's developmental stages (Copple & Bredekamp 2009).

Article   Prepared by: Karen Menke Paciorek, *Eastern Michigan University*

Parent Partnerships: Reciprocal Relationships with Families

CHRISTINE SNYDER

Learning Outcomes

After reading this article, you will be able to:

- Discuss the importance of building and maintaining positive relationships with families.

- Share strategies you could implement that would foster positive working relationships with families.

- Examine your willingness to be open minded to all cultures and backgrounds of families with children in your classroom.

Families establish a unique set of hopes, values, and goals for their children based on love, experience, and instinct. As educators and caregivers, we are invited to be a part of the small circle of people who have a tremendous impact on young children's growth and learning—and, ultimately, their long-term well-being and success.

Working with families is a central component of caring for young children. Yet families and caregivers play unique and appropriately different roles in children's lives. Caregivers are typically responsible for children's care and educational needs during specific times from day to day for the course of a year or two. Families, on the other hand, are responsible for all of children's needs over the course of a lifetime.

These two roles naturally come with different perspectives on goals for the children, as well as different day-to-day expectations. But when we can be open to the unique and valuable insight families provide, the opportunity to work as a team blends the two views to create a positive, whole experience for children. Because young children are dependent on adults to care for them and assist in their learning, a genuine, positive relationship between parents and teachers is essential. More than anyone else, families provide us with valuable information about their child's routines, interests, and preferences. We are dependent on families to offer us insight about how their child interacts with others, engages in a group setting, and communicates.

Building relationships with parents is not without its challenges, though. Each family–caregiver partnership may be facing a different challenge. But anticipating and identifying these challenges can help us work toward a responsive relationship with flexible strategies to focus on meeting the needs of the child in a way that works for each individual family.

From the outset, teachers and caregivers need to intentionally identify strategies that can be used to establish strong, positive family partnerships. A give-and-take, reciprocal relationship with families sets the tone for future interactions and influences the overall success of the child in the group care setting.

Learning by Listening

Relationships between parents and caregivers must be built on trust and the shared belief that we each are acting on the best interests of the children and value input from one another. The best way to establish trust with families is to begin by listening.

The opportunity to build reciprocal trust with parents starts when families first express an interest in your program and come to visit. Making them feel welcome and really listening to their perspectives and questions from the beginning will go a long way. Depending on the children's ages and the goals their parents have for them, parents' concerns could range from sleeping patterns, eating habits, and potty-training to specific developmental goals such as walking, talking, or writing. When you are open to listening to parents and are responsive to their unique needs and concerns, it sets the tone that you value their input and viewpoint.

A dialogue that begins with listening also helps caregivers and administrators learn more about the families in their care. When programs are well-informed about the families they serve, they are more capable of making accommodations, and therefore can provide better service and care to children.

Before the child's first day in the classroom, we can learn about his or her family through dialogue, family questionnaires, and home visits. Home visits allow for a personal, focused connection in which the teachers can interact with the family—including siblings—see the child's favorite home toys, and engage in a one-on-one conversation with the child's parents or primary caregivers about shared goals and expectations for the year. As the year progresses, we can gain valuable insight through many informal and formal channels, such as daily conversations, family events, teacher–family conferences, social media interactions, or simple observations during regular interactions.

Embracing Diversity in the Classroom

Of course, caregivers have their own unique cultural backgrounds and values, and that presents a common challenge in building strong relationships with families. For example, our own experience might lead us to make assumptions about family structures or indicate a value of one type of family structure over another. Teachers who grew up in a two-parent home with a mother and father, for instance, may unintentionally assume or imply that a family has two parents, that they are married, or that there is one man and one woman. In fact, for many years, state-created enrollment forms requested the contact information for the mother and father—an immediate exclusion of homes with two mothers, two fathers, or grandparents providing care for the child. Although our own experiences and values may be different, we should take care not to let our personal biases impact our understanding of families and our ability to establish a positive relationship. Instead, it is important to ask questions, build trust, and learn about families with an open mind.

This is especially important at the outset—that we, as caregivers, are open-minded and willing to build an atmosphere of trust in which families feel comfortable sharing their culture with us, recognizing differences as valuable components that make each of us unique and special.

Once we have overcome the initial challenge of recognizing our biases, the next step is taking positive action to embrace those differences. "We have finally established the essential idea that home cultures and prejudices and discrimination in the larger society deeply affect children's development, and that early childhood programs must address these realities," says Louise Derman Sparks, co-author with Julie Olsen Edwards of *Anti-Bias Education for Young Children and Ourselves.* "The biggest challenge now facing us is to put these basic premises into daily practice in our ECE [early childhood education] organizations and programs."

Understanding a family's unique culture gives us many opportunities to do just that. Incorporating materials that represent children's home lives builds a stronger sense of self and a sense of belonging in the classroom. Including props that children can use to role-play their families' hobbies or jobs allows them to play in ways that are familiar and similar to their home lives. Likewise, including empty food boxes from children's homes or dishes that match what children use in their homes supports children in cooking in the ways that they see their families cook.

Photographs of families are another great way to build familiarity, comfort, and a sense of belonging. Before school begins, you might ask families to supply some pictures that represent important aspects of their culture and members of their family. This may include photos of people who live in the household, places the family travels to frequently, close friends, and family members who live far away.

Photos of children can be placed at each child's cubby so they and their families can easily find their belongings and comfort items. A poster for each child with family photos can be posted around the room at child height so children are able to look at, see, and touch photos of family members throughout the day. Children will also benefit from teacher-made books of family photos in the book area, photos of family members to carry around, or—for infants and toddlers—photo mobiles hanging over diaper-changing areas. These family photos, when placed in a variety of areas throughout the classroom, will make families feel welcome and included in the play space. In addition, opportunities for children to explore family photos will help children become more familiar with the families of their classmates.

Effective Communication with Families

Another common bias we may have, whether personal or cultural, is a preference for certain modes of communication. Establishing trust through dialogue is the foundation of strong relationships with the families we serve. It's imperative, then, that we meet families' needs and preferences when communicating with them about their culture, their values, and their child.

As caregivers, while we are unique individuals, we may have a standard set of strategies that we use with parents: verbal communication at drop-off, monthly written newsletters, text message reminders, and so on. However, when interacting with individual families, we must take *their* personal preferences into consideration. If we overlook the way that families communicate, it's possible that one side or the other is not getting the information that is needed. Parents who speak English as a second language or are not able to read may not understand important messages you send about the program or their child—and they may be afraid to tell you.

Regular communication with parents will help to establish and maintain relationships with families. Common ways of communicating with families include bulletin board postings, text reminders, social media sites, blogs, flyers, e-mail reminders, phone calls, and face-to-face interactions.

While we want to offer information in a variety of forms to meet the needs of all families, it is also important to recognize and accommodate for the individual communication preferences of each family. This may mean that general information for the class is sent via e-mail, with a hard copy included for families who don't use e-mail. For family members who are able to frequently drop off or pick up, bulletin board postings can serve as regular, accessible reminders. Conversely, if families are not in the center frequently because transportation is provided or due to their work hours or location, a different method of communication—such as phone calls, text messages, or e-mails—would be more appropriate.

It's not just the varying modes of communication that present a challenge. It's also finding the time to communicate and connect with families. Due to varying program and family dynamics, many families may find it convenient to touch base at drop-off or pickup times. Other families' work schedules require a friend or nanny to take care of drop-off and pickup. In addition, many families travel for work or serve in the military and are stationed in locations away from their families. "I travel a lot for work," said Bobby Sepulveda, 40. "I appreciate that [my daughter's] teachers take the time to send me a quick email now and then, to communicate something that was important to her. I like to know what's going on at [her] school when I'm gone for weeks at a time, and the fact that her teachers take the time to update me reminds me that she's in good hands."

Even when families are able to be physically present in the environment frequently, it may still be a challenge to engage in meaningful conversation, as both you and the parents are busy tending to children. Again, awareness of these differences between one family and another and a willingness to communicate in ways that accommodate each individual family ensure the openness, respect, and trust that are the necessary foundation of strong family engagement in your program.

Welcoming Families

Just as it's necessary to learn as much as we can about the family life of children in our care, we need to be intentional in providing education to families about our program and what they can expect from their child's experience in group care. The goal of welcoming families includes providing information about the daily routine, program philosophy, and educational goals, as well as the opportunity to meet and interact with the staff. When parents feel informed about their child's experience in a group setting, they will feel more comfortable about their relationship with you and leaving their child in your care.

To start with, it is necessary that the enrollment process and general operating procedures focus on the needs of the family. This includes a thorough orientation process that helps parents learn about the program and about the experiences their children will have during the day. Families should be informed of center policies, such as what will happen in the event of inclement weather or child illness. Staff should also be available to provide information on an individual basis and assist with the school application and enrollment process as necessary.

Families also benefit when caregivers can provide ideas for additional resources in the community. These resources could include developmental screenings, family support groups, financial resources, diagnostic special needs services, or other service referrals as needed. In addition to helping families meet the needs of their child, presenting yourself as a valuable, reliable resource will increase the likelihood that families will be open with you about changes to their child's needs.

Creating Community in Your Classroom

When parents and children first enroll in the program, welcome them by providing a tour of the care space and other important areas such as the child's cubby, parent information boards, and lending libraries. Children and families will feel more comfortable when they can easily navigate the space and find the things they need.

In order to provide information and predictability, there should be a daily schedule posted for parents, as well as a pictorial routine for children that matches the posted routine and is positioned at the child's height. When parents have an idea of what occurs in their child's day, they are better able to make a smooth transition between home and group care, and are able to discuss events in the day that were important to the child. "When I can ask my son about specific times of the daily routine, he's much more willing to reveal details about his day," said Alison Krause, 26. "I like to know what he's been doing, of course, and it gives him another chance to review and make sense of his own day."

Part of any daily routine should be greeting both parents and children in a warm, friendly manner as they arrive. This will ensure a smoother transition and reassure parents about their child being in group care. Welcoming children and families by name lets them know that you value them both as individuals and as an important part of the classroom community. Offering families a place to bottle-feed or nurse their babies' supports their family decisions and individual schedules. Likewise, allowing parents to stay for part of the drop-off transition (if their schedule allows) will assist with children's separation anxiety and also increase parents' familiarity with and sense of belonging in the program. "For my son's first year of pre-school, I participated in greeting and large-group time every day, because I could," said Adam Robson, 42. "A lot of parents don't have the opportunity to do that, but for my son and I, it became a regular, important part of our own daily routine. And it really helped my son overcome his initial anxiety at being away from his parents."

In the event that parents are distressed at drop-off or pickup time, it is important to acknowledge their feelings and offer the support they desire. Parents may benefit from having extended time to stay at the center during these times of day. Or they may simply need your support and your understanding that it can be difficult and emotional to leave a child in group care. How children react to saying goodbye or reuniting with their families may vary, so it is important to be sensitive to children's needs, too. Parents' comfort level at leaving their children often has a significant impact on how children respond to being in group care. The more we can ease parental distress, the more likely we are to help children be comfortable as well.

When families feel they are a part of a community, it strengthens their sense of belonging and connection to all areas of the community. An effective program should include many ways for such connections to be built between families and children, which increases the sense of community as well as promotes a positive sense of self and others. We can build this sense of community through social events in the classroom and by connecting families with common interests. Frequently, families get to know one another during drop-off and pickup times, as well as classroom events. This often leads to play dates or ride sharing to transport children to and from group care.

Parents can also be invited to participate in policy-making committees. Their unique perspectives can contribute to an approach sensitive to meeting the needs of all families. Opportunities for parents to get involved in the center can include volunteering in the classroom, attending evening events for socializing, sharing hobbies or talents as part of a learning experience for children, or attending parent meetings.

The Program-Home Connection

From the start, caregivers should help families feel welcome to participate in the assessment process. It's beneficial for caregivers to include families in initial goal-setting sessions, because that gives an understanding of what families hope their children will learn throughout the year. It also assists caregivers in knowing what kind of information families would like to hear about from day to day.

Each day in a classroom, caregivers take anecdotal notes while playing with children. This information can be used to share stories with families during pickup times and to complete daily notes on children's biological routines and experiences. Families can add to the store of anecdotes collected by caregivers to create a more complete picture of each child's development and to help with intentional planning and formal assessments. This reciprocal exchange can occur informally and day-to-day, in addition to the two or three scheduled conferences each year.

Integral to their child's healthy development in our care is the parents' investment and willingness to make the vital program-home connection. We can do this by informing parents about the curriculum and offering ideas to extend their children's learning at home. This may happen in the form of workshops focusing on various topics in the curriculum, newsletters with tips and suggestions for parents, bulletin boards with content connected to classroom experiences, a resource-lending library for parents to take home information about the curriculum, or play backpacks with tips for interactions to guide parents in play experiences at home. When parents integrate these experiences in a variety of ways in their home, these too become part of the home culture.

Caring for children in their early years is a unique opportunity to engage as a team, with caregivers and family members collaborating to meet both the educational and noneducational needs of the infants and toddlers. We can establish an effective approach to supporting children by initiating a relationship with parents built on trust, taking into consideration differing viewpoints building connections between home and school, and incorporating the importance of family partnerships into all areas of classroom and program practices. When we intentionally plan for strong relationships with families, we ensure a bright, future for all children.

Critical Thinking

1. Practice carefully listening to parents when communicating with them about their children.

2. Think about some strategies that would be effective for developing relationships with families.

3. Plan some ways you could develop a sense of community in your classroom.

Internet References

HighScope Educational Research Foundation Family Engagement
https://highscope.org/families

National Education Association Today
http://neatoday.org/2016/05/23/building-positive-teacher-parent-relationships/

Public Broadcasting Service (PBS)
http://www.pbs.org/parents/education/going-to-school/parent-involvement/parent-teacher-partnership/

Reading Rockets
http://www.readingrockets.org/article/building-parent-teacher-relationships

Article   Prepared by: Karen Menke Paciorek, *Eastern Michigan University*

Connecting with Families

Tips for Those Difficult Conversations

JODI WHITEMAN

Learning Outcomes

After reading this article, you will be able to:

- Name one strategy described by the author that you could use in a conversation with families.
- Describe the role teachers of young children have in supporting families of young children.

K im arrives for her first day as a teacher in a mixed-age infant/toddler classroom at an Early Head Start program. She is excited about this new adventure. She immediately finds that she enjoys working with the babies very much but has trouble communicating with some of their parents, especially when a sensitive concern arises.

On Thursday, her third day on the job, she notices in the morning that 6-month-old Fernando has a terrible diaper rash. When Fernando's mother picks him up that evening, Kim mentions the rash. Fernando's mother says, "That happened at the center. He was fine all weekend and this morning." Kim is confused and worried by this. "Now what do I do?" she asks herself.

The next day 2-year-old Alicia bites another child. Kim later shares with Alicia's father what had happened. He angrily tells her that she obviously is not a good teacher since she could not watch the children to make sure this didn't happen. Kim feels intimidated and tells him she is sorry. That night Kim questions if she has made the right career choice. She knows she loves children, but she never thought working with families would be so hard. She decides to talk to her supervisor, Heath, and get some help from him.

What the Research Tells Us

Many teachers have experiences and feelings like Kim's. Few early childhood professionals enter the field with a strong interest in working with families (Powell 2003). Often early care and education teachers begin their careers without realizing that their work means that they need to partner with families. Teachers may feel unsure and uncomfortable when discussing difficult topics with them (Powell 2003). Both new and seasoned early care and education professionals are eager for help and need a chance to learn strategies and skills, along with practical tools, for holding difficult conversations.

When Kim spoke with Heath, he told her that NAEYC conducted a parent survey to understand parents' perceptions of both center-based child care programs and family child care home providers. The survey asked families whether they turn to program staff for child-related guidance, information, and support (Olson & Hyson 2005). Heath shared two findings from the parent survey that he thought were important for Kim to think about. First, "parents regarded advice giving as intrusive. They preferred to receive information in a cooperative, respectful manner, in the context of a relationship based on a sharing of information. Secondly, parents thought teachers needed more training in parent communication, specifically around communicating about difficult topics".

Heath shared information from another survey that he thought might help Kim. ZERO TO THREE, working with MetLife Foundation and Hart Research Associates, conducted a nationwide parent survey. In the survey, 80 percent of families noted that professionals, including early childhood teachers, either powerfully or moderately influence their decisions regarding their children (Hart Research Associates 2009). Teachers of young children have a significant role in helping and supporting families, yet the teachers themselves need help and support to do so effectively. Talking to Heath, who listened carefully, and getting useful information from him helped Kim realize that she was not alone with her questions and struggles about working with families. Kim felt relieved, supported, and ready to learn more about how to effectively partner with families.

Getting Started

Approaching parents or family members with something they might not want to hear is never easy, especially with the limited time available during drop-off and pickup times. It helps to get to know families well before there is a need to bring up a sensitive topic. That builds a sense of trust and caring that makes it much easier to ask for some time to talk together about a question or concern. Here are some strategies that can help build provider–family relationships. These same strategies can be useful when there is a difficult topic to bring up.

Asking questions and wondering is a strategy that helps providers connect with families. By asking thoughtful questions, teachers honor parents' knowledge of their child. Wondering together with families demonstrates curiosity on the teacher's part, puts the teacher and family member on an equal footing, and demonstrates respect for the family member.

Regarding Fernando's situation, Kim acknowledged to his mother that she might have made a mistake, saying, "I think my question about Fernando's diaper rash got us off to a difficult start. I didn't mean to do that. I just wanted to make sure that you knew about the rash. I thought about what happened and realized that while I was well meaning, I am new here, and we don't even know each other. I hope we can start over. I am wondering if you are available at the end of the day to discuss how to best treat Fernando's diaper rash." Kim might then ask questions such as, "I wonder, has Fernando had a rash like this before?" After listening to his mother's response, she could ask other questions such as, "How did you handle it then?" and "What would you like us to do here?" Kim's asking questions and wondering may help Fernando's mother feel open to participating in the conversation and can go a long way toward building a positive relationship.

Two other strategies that help build relationships with families are active listening and showing empathy. Active listening is listening carefully to what the other person is saying and stating back to them what you understood. This process allows the other person to hear, think about, and clarify her own words. Active listening also involves paying attention to nonverbal messages, such as body language and facial expressions, which help you understand the speaker's meaning. Empathizing involves expressing your understanding and acceptance of another person's experiences and feelings. Teachers can do this by reflecting back what they are seeing and hearing from families; for example, "It can be tough to figure out what to do when your child is acting out. It sounds like this is taking a lot out of you."

Kim decided to use these two strategies to begin building a relationship with Alicia's father. Kim acknowledged to him that she might have gotten off on the wrong foot the day before. Then she expressed empathy for his feelings and used active listening. Kim said, "It sounds like you are really upset about this. I'm sorry this is difficult to hear, and I can understand why it would be! I can imagine that you don't want to hear about Alicia hurting another child. You might even worry if she is somehow in trouble with me. It is typical for children her age to show some aggression when they are frustrated, so I am not upset with her at all. Can I share with you a little bit more about the situation? That way maybe we can better understand what is going on. Then maybe we can find ways to help her so she doesn't end up getting frustrated and biting."

These strategies can help build a foundation of trust, caring, and connection that allows both families and providers to give and receive help, support, and information that benefits young children.

Think About It

- How do you feel when you are challenged in a relationship with a family member? How can you identify your feelings, and can you understand why you may be feeling those emotions?
- Consider a time when someone really listened to you. What did they do to show you they were listening? How did this make you feel? How can you use this experience during difficult conversations that may arise in your work with families?

Try It

- Explore some of the strategies listed in this column, and role-play with your co-worker or supervisor.
- Commit to taking a workshop on establishing relationships with families. Contact your NAEYC Affiliate, www.naeyc.org/affiliates/offices, the local child care resource and referral network (CCR&R), or a community college for professional development opportunities and information about establishing relationships with families.

References

Hart Research Associates. 2009. *Parenting Infants and Toddlers Today: Research Findings.* www.zerotothree.org/about-us/funded-projects/parenting-resources/final_survey_report_3-11-2010.pdf.

Olson, M., & M. Hyson. 2005. "Professional Development. NAEYC Explores Parental Perspectives on Early Childhood Education." *Young Children* 60 (3): 66–68. www.naeyc.org/files/naeyc/file/ecprofessional/STSF_parentsandchildren.pdf.

Powell, D.R. 2003. "Relations between Families and Early Childhood Programs." In *Connecting with Parents in the Early Years,* eds. J. Mendoza, L.G. Katz, A.S. Robertson, & D. Rothenberg, 141–54. Champaign, IL: Early Childhood and Parenting Collaborative, University of Illinois at Urbana–Champaign. http://ecap.crc.uiuc.edu/pubs/connecting.html.

Critical Thinking

1. What are some barriers to having difficult conversations with families?

2. Share two strategies that would be helpful to teachers as they build relationships with families.

Internet References

American Academy of Pediatrics
www.aap.org

Child Welfare League of America (CWLA)
www.cwla.org

Children, Youth and Families Education and Research Network
www.cyfernet.org

Harvard Family Research Project
www.hfrp.org

Teachers Helping Teachers
www.pacificnet.net/~mandel

JODI WHITEMAN, MEd, is the director of the Center for Training Services and Special Projects at ZERO TO THREE. Jodi has worked in the infant/family field for 15 years. jwhiteman@zerotothree.org.

Unit 3

UNIT

Prepared by: Karen Menke Paciorek, *Eastern Michigan University*

Research Practices Affecting the Field

This new unit provides the reader with a few of the most recent research findings affecting young children and their families. The immediate access on our fingertips to new information on an hourly basis means educators have to constantly keep up with the latest reputable research. We can be easily swayed by what we read on our twitter, Facebook, Instagram, or other digital media account that sorting through the massive amount of content we read and hear every day can be overwhelming. Checking the source of the information is a good first step to discerning the validity of the information. A key question to consider as one reads through their daily digital media feed is did the information come from a university, a professional organization, or a government supported study? Studies supported by competitive research funds or those following professional ethical standards have to include more oversight to insure the study is credible. Information from these sources is more reliable than a blog written by someone sitting at their kitchen table.

Professional organizations make it very easy to receive a daily or weekly digital update you can easily scroll through as you go about your day. Some of my favorites are included in the Internet References found at the end of each article.

Early Childhood Educators have a responsibility to keep up with their profession. In fact, one of the defining qualities of a profession versus a job is a profession requires one to participate in ongoing learning about one's chosen field. Being a member of a professional organization, attending a professional development conference, or listening to a webinar while you fold laundry or drive to work can all keep you current on evidence-based practices. Just as we expect those in the health-care field who care for us to constantly improve their knowledge of current best practices, they too expect the same from the educators who care for their children.

We all can remember outstanding teachers from our past and list certain practices by that teacher or administrator that make us remember with great fondness the experiences we had in that school or classroom. There are evidenced-based practices in education that are more successful in helping learners maximize their potential. It is our job to search out the best practices and make sure they are a part of what happens in the

places where we work. Take the initiative to organize a professional learning community at your place of employment. Find an article that addresses an issue the staff are facing and facilitate a discussion of the issue to inform each other and then the families of the children in your care.

Current interest in the effects of technology use, both by children and parents in front of their children, has garnered great interest in the literature. Parents look to educators to help them answer questions about appropriate media use in the home setting and are eager for resources that can guide their decision-making process. Apps are available now that allow for technology to be locked at certain times of the day so uninterrupted family time can take place. Parents need to evaluate their self-discipline and their ability to put the phone down or limit the endless scrolling through twitter or Instagram and focus on family and friends who are present at the time. Many early childhood programs are "phone free zones" so family members can drop off or pick up their children and give them the full attention they need at the beginning or end of the day and not be talking on their phone.

Stress affecting both teachers and children is a frequent topic of research and is worthy of reflection and study. What can teachers do to insure a work environment that is calm and does not cause one to leave at the end of the day with a knot in their stomach? Administrators should constantly be aware of practices that may lead to low morale, high stress and negative interactions between teachers and children. Efforts should be taken to minimize these stressors in the learning environment. Education is a high stress profession for it involves daily work often with others who are unable to fully communicate their needs. Those who spend their days with young children can benefit greatly from a supportive work environment where their efforts are appreciated and valued.

The focus on learning styles of girls and boys is an opportunity for early childhood educators to stop and carefully take stock of the resources available in their classroom for children to explore. If you work in a learning setting, look around and see if there are ample amounts of materials with numerals such as playing cards, calculators, dice, calendars, and menus. Also look for an ample supply of materials for putting things together such as Legos, blocks, blocks that connect, train tracks, along with tools for measuring in a variety of ways. Both boys and girls should be encouraged to interact with all of the materials in the room and if you notice one gender gravitating to certain areas of the room more than the other gender, then see what you can do as a teacher to make the materials inviting for all. Starting at an early age girls do see themselves as less competent and intellectually capable of doing work in the fields requiring math and science skills.

Yes, teaching is complicated work but keeping up with the research helps us make key decisions so we can all provide the very best for the children in our care.

Article Prepared by: Karen Menke Paciorek, *Eastern Michigan University*

How Severe, Ongoing Stress Can Affect a Child's Brain

LINDSEY TANNER

Learning Outcomes

After reading this article, you will be able to:

- Explain how toxic stress and post-traumatic stress disorder differ.
- Discuss how poverty can adversely affect a young child's development and levels of stress.

ASHEVILLE, NC (AP)—A quiet, unsmiling little girl with big brown eyes crawls inside a carpeted cubicle, hugs a stuffed teddy bear tight, and turns her head away from the noisy classroom.

The safe spaces, quiet times, and breathing exercises for her and the other preschoolers at the Verner Center for Early Learning are designed to help kids cope with intense stress so they can learn. But experts hope there's an even bigger benefit—protecting young bodies and brains from stress so persistent that it becomes toxic.

It's no secret that growing up in tough circumstances can be hard on kids and lead to behavior and learning problems. But researchers are discovering something different. Many believe that ongoing stress during early childhood—from grinding poverty, neglect, parents' substance abuse, and other adversity—can smolder beneath the skin, harming kids' brains, and other body systems. And research suggests that can lead to some of the major causes of death and disease in adulthood, including heart attacks and diabetes.

"The damage that happens to kids from the infectious disease of toxic stress is as severe as the damage from meningitis or polio or pertussis," says Dr. Tina Hahn, a pediatrician in rural Caro, Michigan. She says her No. 1 goal as a physician is to prevent toxic stress. Hahn routinely questions families about stresses at home, educates them about the risks and helps them find ways to manage.

Mounting research on potential biological dangers of toxic stress is prompting a new public health approach to identifying and treating the effects of poverty, neglect, abuse, and other adversity. While some in the medical community dispute that research, pediatricians, mental health specialists, educators, and community leaders are increasingly adopting what is called "trauma-informed" care.

The approach starts with the premise that extreme stress or trauma can cause brain changes that may interfere with learning, explain troubling behavior, and endanger health. The goal is to identify affected children and families and provide services to treat or prevent continued stress. This can include parenting classes, addiction treatment for parents, school and police-based programs, and psychotherapy.

Many preschoolers who mental health specialist Laura Martin works with at the Verner Center have been in and out of foster homes or they live with parents struggling to make ends meet or dealing with drug and alcohol problems, depression, or domestic violence.

They come to school in "fight-or-flight" mode, unfocused, and withdrawn or aggressive, sometimes kicking and screaming at their classmates. Instead of adding to that stress with aggressive discipline, the goal is to take stress away.

"We know that if they don't feel safe then they can't learn," Martin said. By creating a safe space, one goal of programs like Verner's is to make kids' bodies more resilient to biological damage from toxic stress, she said.

Many of these kids "never know what's going to come next" at home. But at school, square cards taped at kids' eye level remind them in words and pictures that lunch is followed by quiet time, then a snack, then hand-washing and a nap. Breathing exercises have kids roar like a lion or hiss like a snake to calm them. A peace table helps angry kids work out conflicts with their classmates.

The brain and disease-fighting immune system are not fully formed at birth and are potentially vulnerable to damage from childhood adversity, recent studies have shown. The first three years are thought to be the most critical, and children lacking nurturing parents or other close relatives to help them cope with adversity are most at risk.

Under normal stress situations—for a young child that could be getting a shot or hearing a loud thunderstorm—the stress response kicks in, briefly raising heart rate and levels of cortisol and other stress hormones. When stress is severe and ongoing, those levels may remain elevated, putting kids in a persistent "fight-or-flight" mode, said Harvard University neuroscientist Charles Nelson.

Recent studies suggest that kind of stress changes the body's metabolism and contributes to internal inflammation, which can raise risk for developing diabetes and heart disease. In 2015, Brown University researchers reported finding elevated levels of inflammatory markers in saliva of children who had experienced abuse or other adversity.

Experiments in animals and humans also suggest persistent stress may alter brain structure in regions affecting emotions and regulating behavior. Nelson and others have done imaging studies showing these regions are smaller than usual in severely traumatized children.

Nelson's research on neglected children in Romanian orphanages suggests that early intervention might reverse damage from toxic stress. Orphans sent to live with nurturing foster families before age 2 had imaging scans several years later showing their brains looked similar to those of kids who were never institutionalized. By contrast, children sent to foster care at later ages had less gray matter and their brains looked more like those of children still in orphanages.

Toxic stress is not the same as post-traumatic stress disorder (PTSD). PTSD is a distinct mental condition that can result from an extremely traumatic event, including combat, violence, or sexual abuse. Experts say it can occur in adults and children who live with persistent toxic stress, including children in war-torn countries, urban kids who've been shot or live in violence-plagued neighborhoods, and those who have been physically or sexually abused.

The toxic stress theory has become mainstream, but there are skeptics, including Tulane University psychiatrist Dr. Michael Scheeringa, an expert in childhood PTSD. Scheeringa says studies supporting the idea are weak, based mostly on observations, without evidence of how the brain looked before the trauma.

The American Academy of Pediatrics supports the theory and in 2012 issued recommendations urging pediatricians to educate parents and the public about the long-term consequences of toxic stress and to push for new policies and treatments to prevent it or reduce its effects.

In a 2016 policy noting a link between poverty and toxic stress, the academy urged pediatricians to routinely screen families for poverty and to help those affected find food pantries, homeless shelters, and other resources.

"The science of how poverty actually gets under kids' skin and impacts a child has really been exploding," said Dr. Benard Dreyer, a former president of the academy.

Some pediatricians and schools routinely screen children and families for toxic stress, but it is not universal, said John Fairbank, co-director of the National Center for Child Traumatic Stress. "That's certainly an aspiration. It would be a big step forward," said Fairbank, a Duke University psychiatry professor.

Much of the recent interest stems from landmark U.S. government-led research published in 1998 called the Adverse Childhood Experiences study. It found that adults exposed to neglect, poverty, violence, substance abuse, parents' mental illness, and other domestic dysfunction were more likely than others to have heart problems, diabetes, depression, and asthma.

A follow-up 2009 study found that adults with six or more adverse childhood experiences died nearly 20 years earlier than those with none.

Some children seem resistant to effects from toxic stress. Harvard's Nelson works with a research network based at Harvard's Center on the Developing Child that is seeking to find telltale biomarkers in kids who are affected—in saliva, blood, or hair—that could perhaps be targets for drugs or other treatment to prevent or reduce stress-related damage.

That research is promising but results are likely years off, says Dr. Jack Shonkoff, the center's director.

Alvin and Natalie Clarke brought their young grandchildren into their Cass City, Michigan, home after their parents jailed on drug charges. The 6-year-old grandson hits, yells, breaks toys, and misbehaves in school. His 4-year-old sister used to have nightmares and recoil in fear when her baby doll was left alone on the floor—signs her therapists say suggest memories of neglect.

The Clarkes had never heard the term "toxic stress" when they were granted guardianship in 2015. Now it's a frequent topic in a support group they've formed for other grandparent-guardians.

Their grandson's therapists say he has PTSD and behavior problems likely stemming from toxic stress. Around strangers he's sometimes quiet and polite but the Clarkes say he has frequent tantrums at home and school and threatens his sister. He gets frightened at night and worries people are coming to hurt him, Natalie Clarke said.

Weekly sessions with a trauma-focused therapist have led to small improvements in the boy. The Clarkes say he needs more help but that treatment is costly and his school isn't equipped to offer it.

The little girl has flourished with the help from Early Head Start behavior specialists who have worked with her and the Clarkes at home and school.

"Thank God she doesn't remember much of it," Natalie Clarke said. "She's a happy, loving little girl now."

Critical Thinking

1. What can you do as a teacher to support the emotional needs of young children in your classroom?

2. Develop a list of routines and rituals that are important to establish in a program for young children.

3. Describe some stressors that are present in society that affect children.

Internet References

Alberta Family Wellness Initiative
https://www.albertafamilywellness.org/

Center for Early Childhood Mental Health Consultation
https://www.ecmhc.org/

Southwest Human Development
https://www.swhd.org/

Tanner, Lindsey, "How Severe, Ongoing Stress Can Affect a Child's Brain," The Associated Press, July 12, 2017. Used with permission.

Article   Prepared by: Karen Menke Paciorek, *Eastern Michigan University*

Can Parents' Tech Obsessions Contribute to a Child's Bad Behavior?

BEATA MOSTAFAVI

Learning Outcomes

After reading this article, you will be able to:

- Explain to parents how their excessive time spent on technology can have negative effects on their child's behavior.

- Advocate for parents to reserve certain times of the day or places in the home as free from technology use.

Fatigue. Hunger. Boredom

Those are often on the list of reasons parents mention if their child whines, has tantrums or acts out.

Researchers are now asking if such negative behaviors could be related to something else: parents spending too much time on their smartphones or tablets.

A small study from University of Michigan C.S. Mott Children's Hospital and Illinois State University found that heavy digital technology use by parents could be associated with child behavior issues. The findings were published in the May 2017 online issue of *Child Development*.

Researchers analyzed surveys completed separately by both mothers and fathers from 170 two-parent households. Mothers and fathers were asked about their use of smartphones, tablets, laptops, and other technology—and how the devices disrupted family time (a disturbance that lead author Brandon T. McDaniel coins "technoference.") Interruptions could be as simple as checking phone messages during mealtime, playtime, and routine activities or conversations with their children.

Might a few stolen moments used to check a couple text messages have a deeper effect?

While more research is needed, the study suggests it might: Even low or seemingly normal amounts of tech-related interruption were associated with greater child behavior problems, such as oversensitivity, hot tempers, hyperactivity, and whining.

"This was a cross-sectional study, so we can't assume a direct connection between parents' technology use and child behavior but these findings help us better understand the relationship," says senior author Jenny Radesky, MD, a child behavior expert and pediatrician at Mott. "It's also possible that parents of children with behavioral difficulties are more likely to withdraw or de-stress with technology during times with their child."

But she adds "We know that parents' responsiveness to their kids changes when they are using mobile technology and that their device use may be associated with less-than-ideal interactions with their children. It's really difficult to toggle attention between all of the important and attention-grabbing information contained in these devices, with social and emotional information from our children, and process them both effectively at the same time."

McDaniel, who designed and carried out the study, says researchers hope to learn more about the impact of increasing digital technology use on families and children.

"Research on the potential impact of this exposure lags far behind," says McDaniel, PhD, assistant professor in the Department of Family and Consumer Sciences at Illinois State University.

"It's too early to draw implications that could be used in clinical practice but our findings contribute to growing literature showing an association between greater digital technology use and potential relationship dysfunction between parents and their children."

Parents in the study were asked to rate how problematic their personal device use was based on how difficult it was for them to resist checking new messages, how frequently they worried about calls and texts and if they thought they used their phones too much.

Participants also were asked how often phones, tablets, computers, and other devices diverted their attention when otherwise engaged with their children.

On average, mothers and fathers both perceived about two devices interfering in their interactions with their child at least once or more on a typical day. Mothers, however, seemed to perceive their phone use as more problematic than fathers did.

About half (48 percent) of parents reported technology interruptions three or more times on a typical day while 17 percent said it occurred once and 24 percent said it happened twice a day. Only 11 percent said no interruptions occurred.

Parents then rated child behavior issues within the past two months by answering questions about how often their children whined, sulked, easily got frustrated, had tantrums, or showed signs of hyperactivity or restlessness.

The researchers controlled for multiple factors, such as parenting stress, depressive symptoms, income, parent education as well as co-parenting quality (how supportive partners were of each other in parenting their child), which has been shown to predict child behavior.

The study joins other research and advocacy groups contributing to a larger debate about technology and its effect on child development.

Some professional societies, such as the American Academy of Pediatrics and Zero to Three, recommend "unplugged" family time. But they haven't tested whether lessening or changing digital technology use during parent–child activities is associated with improved child behavior.

McDaniel and Radesky advise parents to try to carve out designated times to put away the devices and focus all attention on their kids.

Reserving certain times of the day or locations as being technology-free—such as mealtime or playtime right after work—may help ease family tensions caused by the modern blurring of outside worlds with home life, they say.

"Parents may find great benefits from being connected to the outside world through mobile technology, whether that's work, social lives, or keeping up with the news. It may not be realistic, nor is it necessary, to ban technology use all together at home," Radesky says. "But setting boundaries can help parents keep smartphones and other mobile technology from interrupting quality time with their kids."

Story Source

Materials provided by **Michigan Medicine—University of Michigan**.

Journal Reference

1. Brandon T. McDaniel, Jenny S. Radesky. Technoference: Parent Distraction with Technology and Associations with Child Behavior Problems. *Child Development*, 2017; doi: 10.1111/cdev.12822

Critical Thinking

1. Observe in a public or home setting how parents' use of technology may take their attention away from their children. What would you say to the parents to encourage less use of technology in-front of their children?

2. What concerns you the most about the following quote from the article? "It's too early to draw implications that could be used in clinical practice but our findings contribute to growing literature showing an association between greater digital technology use and potential relationship dysfunction between parents and their children."

Internet References

Fred Rogers Center Parents Use of Technology
   http://www.fredrogerscenter.org/?s=parents+use+of+technology

Healthy Children.org
   https://www.healthychildren.org/English/family-life/Media/Pages/Tips-for-Parents-Digital-Age.aspx

Parents' Technology Addiction Leads to Behavior Problems in Kids
   http://www.chicagotribune.com/news/ct-parents-technology-addiction-study-met-20170508-story.html

Beata Mostafavi, "Can Parents' Tech Obsessions Contribute to a Child's Bad Behavior?" Michigan Health Lab, Michigan Medicine-University of Michigan, May 24, 2017. http://labblog.uofmhealth.org/lab-report/can-parents-tech-obsessions-contribute-to-a-childs-bad-behavior

Do Girls See Themselves as Less Smart than Boys? Study Says Yes by Lois M. Collins

67

Article

Prepared by: Karen Menke Paciorek, *Eastern Michigan University*

Do Girls See Themselves as Less Smart than Boys? Study Says Yes

Lois M. Collins

Learning Outcomes

After reading this article, you will be able to:

- Discuss the views of girls and boys on intellectual abilities of the sexes.

- Explain some of the cultural dimensions that may affect one's perception of their abilities.

Little girls may stereotype themselves out of education and career options, according to a study.

At age 5, both boys and girls saw themselves as smart. By age 6, when asked who was "brilliant," both boys and girls selected males, researchers found. Asked to choose between work that required brilliance and work that required effort, the girls sorted themselves into the hard-work tasks.

"We found this stereotyping at a very young age and we also found this association has immediate impact on activities boys and girls are interested in," said lead author Lin Bian, from the University of Illinois at Champaign, who co-authored the study with researchers from New York University and Princeton.

Published in the journal Science, the study concluded stereotypes that "associate high-level intellectual ability" with men more than women "discourage women's pursuit of many prestigious careers."

Bian noted some of the high-paying jobs at stake require high-level mental ability, such as physics or engineering. "It's important to know if young women and girls are held back from pursuing these jobs because of the stereotypes they are exposed to," she said. "If they don't learn early that they are capable and smart, then by the time they reach adulthood and are in a position to decide on a career, it could be hard for them to catch up."

Young Stereotypes

For the first part of the research, children were read a story about someone who is "really, really smart," then asked to pick from pictures of two men and two women who they think that person is. At age 5, boys and girls were both inclined to select someone of their own gender. By age 6, both selected a male as the smart person.

Girls said that female students were more likely to get good grades than male students. But instead of associating that with intellectual ability, they credited hard work.

The researchers then offered children two games from which to choose. One, the children were told, is "for children who are really, really smart," while the other is for "children who try really, really hard." The boys most often picked the game for smart children, while girls picked the game for hard-working children—a choice Bian suggests reflects less confidence in intellectual skills.

Research from Brigham Young University last summer noted a similar potential chilling effect from gender stereotypes young children absorb. Little girls who embrace "princess culture" could sell themselves short when it comes to believing in their own capabilities. That study was published in the journal Child Development.

"Feminine behavior can be great on so many dimensions, like being kind and nurturing," lead author Sarah Coyne, an associate professor of human development in BYU's School of Family Life, told the Deseret News. "But girls can be limited by stereotypes in a number of ways. They can think they can't do well in math and science or they don't want a career."

The difference in the responses between age 5 and 6 in the recently published Science study was somewhat startling, but the researchers noted that children at early school ages begin to learn about the social world around them. "Identifying whether it's because of parents, schools, peers, media, or something else—well, there are so many factors and we're failing to figure this out," said Bian.

Very young children have a "wonderful egocentrism," said clinical psychologist Stephanie O'Leary of Mount Kisco, New York, who was not involved in this research. "They see and identify with all this good stuff within themselves." But by first grade, they're more likely to see intellectual good stuff in the boys, not the girls, she added.

Bian said looking into the sources that lead to stereotyping is an important next step for the researchers.

Combatting Stereotypes

Parents, teachers, coaches, and others should be "mindful of the way we talk about intelligence and the way we communicate to our children," said O'Leary.

Parents have many opportunities to call attention to bright females. If a parent is reading a book to young children, he or she can comment on how clever or smart the writer is. It's not pitting men and women against each other, but rather noting that both genders are smart and capable.

People need to pay attention to their own unconscious biases, too, she said. It's not uncommon for folks to assume that a doctor or an attorney they haven't met is a man. It's easy to ask and then get it right when speaking to kids about that person.

Women should examine how they present themselves to children, said O'Leary. It's not about bragging, but it is important that children see women's intellect, reasoning skills, and dedication. "It's bragging when you beat it to death. It's fact-checking when you say, 'I had a great idea and it helped us get everything we needed done.'"

Men also need to point out examples of bright, capable women. "It is very powerful for boys and girls to hear their fathers point out brilliance in women and to hear their fathers discuss why stereotyping is problematic," said O'Leary.

She said she was pleased that young girls identified with being hard workers in the study. That demonstrates their resilience, she said. "In the long haul, that's more protective than being brilliant. When you're choosing to do things (designed) for smart kids, if you fail, you could take it you're not smart. If hard workers fail, it just means they have to keep working. These girls have spitfire and tenacity."

Critical Thinking

1. Observe teachers communicating with young children for signs of different tones, vocabulary, or levels of encouragement given to boys and girls. Why do you think this may happen?

2. What can parents and teachers do to raise competent and confident children of both sexes?

Internet References

Girls in STEM
   http://www.gstemdenver.org/

Girls in Tech
   https://girlsintech.org/

Raising a Powerful Girl
   http://www.pbs.org/parents/parenting/raising-girls/body-image-identity/raising-a-powerful-girl/

LOIS M. COLLINS is a reporter and columnist for the *Deseret News*.

Collins, Lois M., "Do Girls See Themselves as Less Smart than Boys? Study Says Yes," *Deseret News*, February 15, 2017. Used with permission.

Article   Prepared by: Karen Menke Paciorek, *Eastern Michigan University*

New Report from SRCD on What PreK-3rd Means for Instruction

ANNA SILLERS

Learning Outcomes

After reading this article, you will be able to:

- Explain the importance of instructional continuity from Pre-K to primary learning.

- Describe how social and emotional development can improve through curriculum and instruction that is aligned and cohesive.

- List ways educators can create academic continuity in their school.

In a recent Society for Research in Child Development report "PK-3: What Does it Mean for Instruction?" authors, and members of the DREME Network, explain the many benefits of continuity of instruction and classroom management and offer ideas for how districts and schools can achieve it. (The DREME Network is a group of researchers dedicated to advancing early math education.)

While more and more elementary schools are offering pre-K, well-aligned curricula and instruction between pre-K and the early grades have not necessarily followed. The authors explain why instructional continuity should be made a priority and how it can help students both academically and socially. In their report, the authors write that children follow "fairly predictable learning trajectories" when developing an understanding of particular math topics.When teachers know their students' learning trajectories, teachers are better able to identify the next learning topic and develop instruction just beyond a student's current conceptual knowledge. This is also true for reading comprehension and other subjects.

Additionally, instructional continuity from one grade to another helps students develop a deeper understanding of previous knowledge. For example, when a student learns only one set of rules to solve a math problem, he or she may incorrectly use these rules with other questions. When skills are practiced in different contexts, students often gain more adaptive and flexible skills, such as understanding math concepts or reading comprehension, and are more likely to transfer these skills to other settings. "When experiences are disconnected, students have difficulty incorporating new understandings into prior knowledge and altering prior knowledge when necessary," the authors write.

There are also social and emotional benefits for students who receive well-aligned instruction. When curricula between pre-K and third grade are aligned, students are better able to watch themselves master skills over time, making them more likely to build confidence and motivation in their abilities.

It may also be helpful to align classroom management practices and expectations across grade levels. Changing the rules each year can be confusing and takes away from instruction, the authors explained. By establishing routines for gaining students' attention and exiting the classroom, for example, teachers can skip reteaching new rules each year. This is especially true for English language learners: consistent routines year-to-year can help English learners learn the language more quickly.

Two major players in achieving continuity in the classroom are schools and districts. The report outlined five ways these institutions can create academic continuity:

- Investing in professional development continuity across grades.
- Aligning formative assessments and data systems.
- Emphasizing socioemotional development in kindergarten.
- Creating a coherent instructional framework for other school practices besides academics.
- Developing and implementing an aligned curriculum across grades.

By investing in professional development continuity for teachers between pre-K and third grade, school districts can help bring these teachers together to understand the typical developmental trajectories of children. For some teachers, these learning trajectories may be a new concept. Additionally, for teachers to provide coherent and aligned academic instruction, they must understand the structure and interconnections of the subjects they teach. Through professional development, teachers can gain a better grasp of the material to help their students build on previous knowledge and skills. Professional development across grade levels can also lead to better communication and collaboration among teachers, which has been found to improve the quality of instruction. When teachers are knowledgeable about the grades before and after the grade they teach, they will better be able to provide continuous instruction.

Additionally, using assessments and data systems, such as Kindergarten Readiness Assessments, can lead to continuity by providing teachers with information that can be used for adjusting instruction. An assessment system in New Jersey, for example, includes progress indicators that are aligned from pre-K through third grade with the skills that students are and are not attaining, allowing teachers to prepare accordingly and create individualized plans to help students meet the standards.

In addition to promoting continuity academically, schools can also create continuity of social–emotional skills. Some in the early childhood field worry that creating continuity between pre-K and elementary school will "push down" negative practices such as limiting time for social–emotional development and play. But simply "pushing up" good pre-K practices into kindergarten isn't ideal either. Instead, the authors explain that a solution would involve "changes in both directions." For stronger continuity between pre-K and the early grades, both an increased emphasis on appropriate academic learning opportunities in pre-K and on social and emotional development in K-3rd will likely be necessary.

Schools can also create a coherent instructional framework, or a set of guides and practices for school-level decisions such as hiring and evaluating teachers, to improve student achievement. One study, included in the DREME Network report,

found that schools with a coherent instructional framework and that allocate resources toward the school's common instructional framework have higher student achievement than schools without coherent instructional frameworks between pre-K and third grade.

Lastly, schools and school districts can develop and implement the same curriculum across grades from pre-K through third grade to improve continuity. Unsurprisingly, one study found that "preschools that adopted a packaged curriculum were more continuous with kindergarten than preschools that did not use a curriculum." However, the DREME network authors stressed that a packaged curriculum does not necessarily guarantee continuity in instruction, nor is it required for continuity in instruction. It is important for teachers to be responsive to student needs and adjust their instruction accordingly.

The PreK-3rd movement continues to grow. As more school districts and schools take steps to provide a seamless educational experience for children from pre-K through third grade, they would be wise to focus on what it means for instruction.

Critical Thinking

1. What does the author mean by "push down and Pushing up" of practices and what does she recommend instead?

2. Think about the factors, such as children moving frequently, that could complicate the instruction process. What recommendations would you make as a result of reading this article?

Internet References

Human Capital Research Collaborative
http://hcrc.umn.edu/

National Institute for Early Education Research
http://nieer.org/

The Importance of Continuity for Children Birth through Age 8
https://www.nap.edu/read/19401/chapter/11

ANNA SILLERS was an intern with New America's Early and Elementary Education department.

Sillers, Anna, "New Report from SRCD on What PreK-3rd Means for Instruction," *New America*, April 17, 2017.

Article   Prepared by: Karen Menke Paciorek, *Eastern Michigan University*

Even with More Research, Many Q's Remain about QRIS

ABBIE LIEBERMAN

Learning Outcomes

After reading this article, you will be able to:

- Explain how QRIS were made a key priority by the federal government for early childhood programs.

- Discuss why the Improvement (I) part of a QRIS is often overlooked.

As researchers have learned more about the importance of quality in early care and education (ECE) in recent years, policy makers have been trying to figure out how to best raise the caliber of programs. The primary policy solution in almost all states has been to create Quality Rating and Improvement Systems (QRISs) that evaluate the quality of ECE programs based on a common set of metrics established by the state.

The logic behind these systems goes like this: ECE programs earn ratings, parents can use these ratings to tell which programs are high quality (recent research shows they may not be able to tell on their own), parents will choose to send their children to better programs, and ECE programs with low ratings will take steps to improve their quality in order to keep up enrollment as they respond to market demands. And then, the ultimate goal—improving child outcomes—will be achieved. At least in theory.

As Jill Cannon and her colleagues at RAND explain in a recent policy paper, there are many assumptions in that logic model that do not always hold true. Unexpected complications arise with most policy solutions, especially in the early stages of implementation, and QRISs are no exception.

According to RAND, 49 states have a QRIS either implemented or in the planning or piloting stages. While these accountability systems already existed in some states prior to 2008, the Obama administration accelerated their implementation by making them a key priority in Race to the Top-Early Learning Challenge (RTT-ELC). To be eligible for close to one billion dollars in competitive RTT-ELC funding, states needed to use or create a QRIS with multiple tier levels reflecting varying program quality. Federal and state officials made massive investments in QRISs, even though there was actually limited research around the effectiveness of these systems at the time.

A lot more research on QRIS effectiveness has recently become available; however, thanks to a requirement that RTT-ELC grantees conduct a validation study to determine whether their tiers accurately reflect meaningful differences in program quality and whether different levels of quality lead to different child outcomes. QRIS validation studies have been published in 11 states so far: California, Colorado, Delaware, Indiana, Maine, Minnesota, Missouri, Oklahoma, Pennsylvania, Virginia, and Wisconsin. Unfortunately, it's still somewhat unclear whether benefits of these systems outweigh the costs in their current form. RAND's review of the validation studies found some progress in developing valid rating systems, but concludes that "evidence is still quite limited and often contradictory, preventing firm conclusions about the validity of QRIS ratings as currently designed." Validation studies found that QRIS ratings are related to "one or more independent measures of program quality" but relationships were modest and the differences in quality between tiers were usually small. Several studies also showed a positive relationship between QRIS ratings and child outcomes in at least one domain, but again, relationships tend to be weak and limited. The RAND authors do note potential limitations from some of the validation studies because some QRISs were still being implemented or had limited programs participating.

As RAND explains, when QRISs were first being designed, early child experts were using the information they had available to design the best systems. But experts knew little at the time about which quality indicators actually support child development, how to weigh different indicators, and how much it would cost programs to implement certain requirements.

There's been more research on what is needed for a high-quality program in recent years. Unfortunately, what matters most is difficult to measure. For instance, research shows that having a curriculum is essential. It's easy to check a box on whether a program has a curriculum in place, or even a developmentally appropriate curriculum. It's more difficult to measure whether a program is implementing that curriculum well. Fidelity of implementation is the essential component. We also know that learning for young children depends largely on the quality of interactions and relationships they have with adults. Measuring the quality of adult–child interactions is costly and time consuming.

Another aspect of the QRIS that often gets overlooked is the "I" or improvement component. There is limited research on what types of supports are most effective for helping programs improve quality. Many QRISs offer multiple types of supports and interventions, including research-supported options like coaching, as well as options with no research base, such as peer-supported activities. Individualized coaching is one of the few types of professional learning that is shown to work, but again, it is expensive and time intensive.

While there have been challenges with designing QRISs to best measure quality and support improvement, there have also been unexpected complications that defy the original logic of the intervention. For instance, many Americans live in childcare deserts where there are extremely limited childcare options, regardless of quality. Implementing a QRIS doesn't mean more childcare centers appear. Some providers also don't feel incentivized to join the QRIS because they already have full enrollment, even if they are low quality. Parents also sometimes choose to stay in a program that may be considered low quality because it appeals to them for other reasons, such as proximity to home or work. Other programs may want to improve but lack the resources to do so. Many states do offer higher reimbursement rates for participating providers that accept childcare subsidies, but sometimes the higher rate is not enough to justify the cost of making the quality improvements.

Across the country, state officials have invested a great deal of time and money in this policy intervention with the hope of improving child outcomes. More research is needed to determine how to effectively and efficiently measure program quality and how to support programs as they try to improve. States must be willing to use the results of validation studies and other research to refine these rating systems if they want to see meaningful results.

Critical Thinking

1. Discuss why some early childhood providers are reluctant to use a QRIS.
2. What QRIS is used in your state? Talk to a teacher in an early childhood program and ask how the rating system has impacted their work with young children.

Internet References

Overview of the QRIS Resource Guide
https://qrisguide.acf.hhs.gov/files/QRIS_Resource_Guide_2015.pdf

QRIS Resource Guide
https://qrisguide.acf.hhs.gov/index.cfm?do=qrisabout

Quality Rating and Improvement Systems
http://www.buildinitiative.org/TheIssues/EarlyLearning/QualityQRIS.aspx

ABBIE LIEBERMAN is a policy analyst with the Education Policy program at New America. She is a member of the Early & Elementary Education Policy team, where she provides research and analysis on policies that impact children from birth through third grade.

Lieberman, Abbie, "Even with More Research, Many Q's Remain about QRIS," *New America*, June 2, 2017.

Article   Prepared by: Karen Menke Paciorek, *Eastern Michigan University*

How Teachers' Stress Affects Students: A Research Roundup

Sarah D. Sparks

Learning Outcomes

After reading this article, you will be able to:

- Describe how high levels of stress in teachers can affect their students' level of stress.

- Name the effective teaching strategies listed in the article that may not be observed in classrooms with teachers showing higher levels of stress in the beginning of year.

New research is helping to clarify how teachers become chronically stressed, and how it can affect their students' well-being and achievement.

"Relationships really matter for learning; there's a lot of evidence around that," said Robert Whitaker, a professor of public health and pediatrics at Temple University.

In one 2016 study, University of British Columbia researchers tracked the levels of stress hormones of more than 400 elementary students in different classes. They found teachers who reported higher levels of burnout had students with higher levels of the stress hormone cortisol each morning, suggesting classroom tensions could be "contagious."

For example, researchers from the University of Groningen in the Netherlands interviewed a small pool of 143 beginning teachers over the course of a year. Those who showed higher levels of stress at the beginning of the year displayed fewer effective teaching strategies over the rest of the school year, including clear instruction, effective classroom management, and creation of a safe and stimulating classroom climate for their students, than did the teachers with lower initial stress levels.

Meanwhile, the University of Virginia is conducting one of the first long-term experimental studies of how classroom-management techniques affect teachers' stress and effectiveness in instruction. Researchers from the university's YouthNex research center and the Center for Advanced Study of Teaching and Learning randomly assigned nearly 200 early-career to normal district training or training in the Good Behavior Game, a research-backed social–emotional-learning program in which teachers reward students' positive group behaviors. Teachers who used the game also had one-on-one video coaching every two to three weeks for a year, to help them identify their own stress levels and ways they can improve their interactions with students.

How Teachers See Stress

So what makes a classroom normal for one teacher and stressful to another? The University of Texas at Austin researchers, led by psychology professor Chris McCarthy, found that the answer depends on whether teachers feel they have the cognitive and other resources to meet their students' needs.

The researchers used federal Schools and Staffing Survey data to create profiles of the "demands" on teachers, based on their and their students' background characteristics; whether their classes had high proportions of English-learners, students with disabilities, or students in poverty; and whether their racial group made up a minority of those in the school. They then compared those demands to teachers' reported resources and whether the teachers felt they had autonomy in their classrooms. Teachers whose demands were greater than their perceived resources were only half as likely to say they would choose to become teachers again as were teachers who saw their demands and resources as balanced. Teachers who reported more resources than demands (a smaller group) were more than twice as likely as teachers with "balanced demands and resources" to say they would become teachers again and would return to their district next year.

"This is purely about perceived demand and resources; two teachers in the same school and teaching the same kids could feel they have more or less resources," said Richard Lambert, who cowrote the study. But, he added, individual schools often had very different concentrations of the most high-need students in different classrooms. "That's something that administrators absolutely have control over. If I'm a 4th grade teacher, and there are three others down the hall, we all know five minutes [into the school year] that Ms. Jones got dealt a much harder hand this year. The perception of whether you feel treated fairly by your principal is enormous" in its relation to teacher stress.

Critical Thinking

1. Reflect on the stressor that could lead teachers to have less effective classroom teaching strategies.

2. What are strategies that could assist teachers in de-stressing and bringing a more focused approach to their teaching.

Internet References

Stress Busting Tips for Teachers
https://www.scholastic.com/teachers/articles/teaching-content/15-stress-busting-tips-teachers/

Stress Signs in Teachers
https://www.tes.com/articles/12-signs-stress

Teachers Are Stressed and That Should Stress Us All
http://www.npr.org/sections/ed/2016/12/30/505432203/teachers-are-stressed-and-that-should-stress-us-all

Unit 4

UNIT

Prepared by: Karen Menke Paciorek, *Eastern Michigan University*

Diverse Learners

This unit focuses on the many diverse learners who attend our early childhood programs and schools. In the graduate early childhood seminar, I teach for students earning their Master's degree in ECE; we have many lengthy discussions about the numbers of children the students encounter on a daily basis with a Sensory Processing Disorder, an Obsessive-Compulsive disorder, as well as those with a diagnosis of Autism Spectrum Disorder. The graduate students, many of whom are full-time teachers of young children from the ages of 2 to 8, were seeking help from the professional literature, each other, and other professionals to best assist them as they learned about the effects these disorders can have on a child's ability to learn and function as a contributing member of the classroom community. Educators of young children are increasingly called on to assist families as they help navigate the choppy waters they face with a child who is displaying behaviors not found in typically developing children. We must continue to educate ourselves about the services available and strategies that can help the child become a part of the home and school environment in ways that will lead to a productive life.

If we want students to perform at a high level we must have high expectations for behavior, academic achievement, and future goals. When educators fail to provide the support to students that will allow them to achieve, both now and in the future we fail in our job. Who are we to determine after a brief assessment or one test the fate of a child's educational experience for the rest of his or her time in school? We must not underestimate ability and hold all teachers and students to high standards and constantly encourage everyone to succeed. An educated population is better for all of us and insuring from the very beginning that all children have the necessary skills to be successful learners benefits all of society. It is less expensive to provide children early with the skills they will need and the resources to be successful learners than to provide remedial help for 13 years of education and beyond.

Another issue with deep implications for the early childhood profession is how we care for and educate children in inclusive environments. Nationwide, college, and university programs are incorporating the standards from the National Association for the Education of Young Children (NAEYC) and Council for Exceptional Children (CEC) into their programs. The standards require programs educating teachers at two- and four-year institutions to include content and field experiences on working with

children, especially children with disabilities in inclusive environments. As teacher preparation institutions address the standards in their course content, there will be more teachers out in the field better equipped to meet the needs of special needs children and their families. The standards are all encompassing in their focus on the diversity and richness in the children and families we serve. Recruiting and retaining qualified teachers who are well prepared to work with all children in environments established to be inclusive and differentiated is the new normal in schools. Preservice teachers need many experiences in settings serving diverse learners. This can be challenging for teacher preparation institutions located in communities lacking diversity. Educated students with limited experience traveling to other cultures or interacting with children and families who are different from themselves must supplement their own experiences to be successful teachers and be able to meet the needs of all children and families. Assess your prior experiences with children and families and see if you need to volunteer or work in settings different from your upbringing or past work to better equip yourself with skills needed to work with all families and children. We tend to gravitate to familiar and comfortable experiences, but good teachers stretch themselves to become familiar with the life experiences children in their class bring to the learning environment. Spend some time with a family who has a child with a disability. Get to know the stresses that child as well as the parents and other siblings may deal with on a day-to-day basis. If you own a car and many of your families depend on public transportation, take the bus one day to more fully understand the frustrations that can come from depending on a fixed schedule. Shop for groceries in the local markets used by the families in your classroom. In short, really get to know the many different life experiences the families you work with face in their daily lives.

It is our job to develop the relationships with families necessary to find out that Nora, the one-year-old new to your classroom, is growing up in a bilingual home and that her mother and maternal grandparents communicate with her in Romanian and her father and her paternal grandparents speak English. Help Nora, and all of the other dual language learners (DLL) in your care, feel comfortable as they work to master both the written and spoken languages. It is reported that 80 percent of DLL children are learning Spanish and English. It is also worthy to note there are increasingly more children who are tri-language learners like Evelyn, the young daughter of one of my former students, whose father speaks Spanish, her mother English, and she is living in Shanghai, China. Recognize a DLL versus an English language learner (ELL), one who has competence in communicating in their first language and is now working to master English as a second language to be a successful learner in American schools. Currently, approximately 17 percent of children attending school in large cities are ELLs but that number is expected to grow to 40 percent by 2050. Be knowledgeable on how you can best support the language learning and development for both types of English learners.

Exploring issues related to diverse learners serves as a reminder to all teachers that individualizing learning can be accomplished through a thoughtful and intentional approach. All educators, but especially those who work with young children, need familiarity with response to intervention and the steps educators can take to as my Great Aunt Nene used to say, "do a stitch in time to save nine." Early prevention is one of the cornerstones of our profession. The strong foundation we build early in a child's life will serve him or her well into the future. We know that if we can intervene early and work with the child and family, we can help that child get on track and compete with peers. The increase of preschool suspension and expulsion is an example of an issue educators can tackle and cooperate to find solutions to help children before their behavior identifies them and causes learning and behavioral issues throughout life.

There are more and more examples of teachers adjusting their image of diverse learners and families. Only when all educators are accepting of the wide diversity that exists in family structures and among individual children will all children feel welcomed and comfortable to learn at school. The collaboration of families, the community, and school personnel will enable children to benefit from the partnership these three groups bring to the educational setting. The articles in this unit represent many diverse families and children and the issues surrounding young children today. An open mind and tolerance for families that may not be of the same composition as your own will allow educators to support all learners.

Article   Prepared by: Karen Menke Paciorek, *Eastern Michigan University*

ADHD: From Stereotype to Science

Forget Dennis the Menace and other outdated stereotypes about kids with ADHD. New research reveals the breadth and complexity of the disorder.

THOMAS E. BROWN

Learning Outcomes

After reading this article, you will be able to:

- Share some of the differences in brain development and connectivity between a child diagnosed with ADHD and a child not diagnosed with ADHD.

- Explain to a parent who has a child diagnosed with ADHD the genetic link.

- List some of the characteristics found in an individual diagnosed with ADHD and how those may affect executive functioning.

In almost every classroom, at least one or two students are identified as having attention deficit hyperactivity disorder (ADHD). Sometimes the parents mention at the start of the term that their child has been diagnosed with ADHD; sometimes word comes from a 504 plan or a teacher who previously had that student in class. Usually the ADHD label is taken as a warning that the student is likely to be difficult to teach and manage, that he or she will be more restless and disruptive than most other students in the class.

However, this image of the student with ADHD as Dennis the Menace is an outdated stereotype. Some students with ADHD *are* restless and disruptive, but many others with this disorder are quieter, more distracted and passive, and not very productive or consistent in their work.

Ever since it was first described in the medical literature in 1902, the disorder, now referred to as ADHD, has been considered essentially a behavioral problem. For a long time, it was seen as just a problem of hyperactive little boys who couldn't sit still, wouldn't stop talking, and frustrated their parents and teachers with chronic misbehavior. The term *attention deficit* wasn't added to the name until 1980. Since then, there have been substantial changes in our scientific understanding of ADHD that are important for educators to know.

An Update on the Basic Facts

These facts are now well established in the scientific research.

- ADHD is a developmental impairment of the brain's self-management system that includes problems with getting motivated, organized, and started on necessary tasks; focusing on what needs to be attended to and shifting focus when needed; managing alertness and sleep; sustaining effort to complete tasks; processing and outputting information efficiently; managing emotions; using short-term working memory; and monitoring one's actions to fit the setting and avoid excessive impulsivity (see Figure 1).

- All of us experience characteristics of ADHD from time to time; those with ADHD simply have more chronic and impairing difficulty with these problems. ADHD isn't an all- or -nothing situation like pregnancy, where one either is or isn't pregnant. ADHD is more like depression—it comes in small, medium, and large levels of severity. Everyone feels down sometimes, but being unhappy for a couple of days doesn't warrant a diagnosis of clinical depression. The diagnosis is reserved for those who are significantly and persistently impaired by their symptoms.

- Although some children and adults with ADHD have significant problems with hyperactive and excessively impulsive behavior, many with the disorder don't display

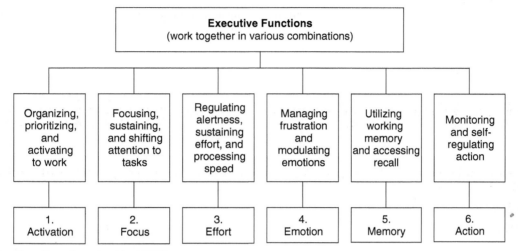

Figure 1   Executive Functions Impaired in ADHD

Sources: From *Attention Deficit Disorder: The Unfocused Mind in Children and Adults* (p. 22), by Thomas E. Brown, 2005, New Haven: Yale University Press. Copyright © 2005 by Thomas E. Brown.

such behavior. The majority of those who were "hyper" as children outgrow most of their hyperactivity in early adolescence but continue to have chronic difficulty with inattention and related problems.

- ADHD is highly heritable; it runs in families. Twenty-five percent of children with ADHD have a parent with ADHD, and 30 percent have a brother or sister with ADHD. Twenty studies comparing identical twins yielded a heritability index of 0.75, which means that most of the variability in developing ADHD is accounted for not by family environment but by inherited vulnerabilities (Faraone et al., 2005). Subsequent studies have demonstrated that this vulnerability isn't caused by any one gene; it's caused by a large number of genes in combination.

- Longitudinal and other imaging research has demonstrated significant differences in brain development and connectivity of children with ADHD compared with typically developing children of similar age (Shaw et al., 2007). Although much brain development is similar in the two groups, some areas of the brain that are important for self-management tend to mature about three to five years later in those with ADHD.

- It was once thought that a child with ADHD would outgrow the disorder before reaching the age of about 14. However, longitudinal studies have shown that approximately 70 percent of those who have ADHD in childhood will continue to have some ADHD impairments at least into late adolescence (Biederman, Petty, Evans, Small, & Faraone, 2010; Biederman, Petty,

Monuteaux, et al., 2010.) For many but not all, the impairments of ADHD continue throughout life.

- ADHD is sometimes apparent during the preschool years, but it's often not noticeable until the child enters elementary school or advances into middle school, where there's no longer just one teacher who provides structure and control for most of the day. Some children don't demonstrate significant ADHD impairments until they enter high school or move away from home and must deal with challenges of more independent life in college or employment. Those with later onset of ADHD can be fully as impaired as those with earlier onset.

- ADHD has nothing to do with how intelligent a person is. ADHD is found in people across the full range of intellectual abilities.

- Emotions play two important roles in ADHD, neither of which is reflected in current diagnostic criteria. First, conscious and unconscious emotions play a crucial role in the problems of motivation and self-regulation that are pervasive in ADHD. Second, many people with ADHD have chronic difficulty recognizing and managing the expression of their emotions.

- ADHD is not just one or two specific symptoms. It's a complex syndrome, a cluster of impairments that often appear together, although some aspects of the disorder may be more or less prominent in any particular person. There are many differences among those with ADHD, even among those of similar age; people with the disorder are not all alike in either their strengths or their difficulties.

- Most people with ADHD also have difficulties resulting from one or more co-occurring disorders. The incidence of learning disorders, anxiety and mood disorders, sleep disorders, obsessive–compulsive disorders, substance use disorders, and autism spectrum disorders is considerably higher among those with ADHD than in the general population. Sometimes the co-occurring disorder is recognized, whereas the ADHD is not.
- Medication doesn't cure the disorder, but for about 8 of 10 people with ADHD, carefully managed medication significantly improves the symptoms. These medications aren't like an antibiotic that may cure an infection; they're more like eyeglasses that improve vision while they're worn.

The Central Mystery of ADHD

There's one fact about ADHD that's most puzzling: The symptoms are situationally variable. That is, people who struggle with chronic ADHD problems may have none of those problems when they engage in a particular activity or task.

Although they struggle to focus on their schoolwork, students with ADHD may demonstrate a remarkable ability to focus and work effectively when they're playing a sport, creating art or music, doing mechanical tasks, or playing a favorite video game.

Although they may not be able to keep directions for assignments in mind or retain basic facts learned in social studies or math, they may have an incredible ability to recall the statistics about their favorite baseball team or the lyrics of popular songs.

When asked why they can focus so well when it comes to these few activities, students with ADHD often reply that it depends on whether the task is interesting—that if it's not, they just can't stay tuned. Although this may be true for everyone—that we focus better on things that interest us—there's an important difference here. Most of us can make ourselves focus on something we recognize as important, even though it's pretty boring. For those with ADHD, doing so is much more difficult.

A patient once remarked to me that having ADHD "is like having erectile dysfunction of the mind. If the task you're trying to do is something that really interests you, you can perform. But if the task you are trying to do is not intrinsically interesting, you can't make it happen." Although ADHD often appears to be a problem with willpower, it's not. It's a problem with the dynamics of the chemistry of the brain.

When people are faced with a task that really interests them—because it appears to offer pleasure to them *at that moment* or seems to ward off some imminent unpleasantness they want to avoid—that perception, conscious, or unconscious,

instantly changes the chemistry of the brain. This motivation process is *not* under our voluntary control.

ADHD and Reading

The motivation problem is often apparent in reading. Students with ADHD often report that they may understand a text as they read it—they can decode all the words and understand what's being said. Yet just a few minutes later, they don't have the foggiest idea what they just read. To extract the meaning of the text and retain it, they often have to reread it several times. One student with ADHD reported,

> When I'm reading something that's not really interesting to me, it's like I'm licking the words and not chewing them. I know what all the words mean as I'm reading them, but they just don't stick inside my head. I don't really digest them. That's why I have to write notes while I'm reading or use a highlighter or else just read the same page over several different times.

ADHD and Memory

Many students with ADHD have adequate or even exceptionally good long-term storage memory. They may be able to recite extended song lyrics or explain in detail the storyline of a movie they saw years ago. Yet they may have great difficulty keeping in mind the directions the teacher just gave for an assignment. During class discussions, students with ADHD may raise their hands to answer a question the teacher has posed and then forget what they intended to say if the teacher calls on someone else first.

Their problem isn't with long-term storage memory; the memory problem in ADHD is more with short-term working memory, the ability to keep one bit of information in mind while thinking about or doing something else.

Students with ADHD will sometimes study for a test the night before the test is given. A parent may quiz them until they have all the material clearly in mind. They walk into class the next day expecting to get a really good grade, only to find that a big chunk of what they knew so well the night before has suddenly evaporated. They can't recall the information when they need it for the test, but a few hours or days later, something jogs their memory and the information is back again.

It's not that the students hadn't learned it; they simply weren't able to retrieve the information from memory when they needed it. Working memory is the search engine of the brain. Those with ADHD often suffer from chronic difficulties with their working memory even though their longer-term storage memory works very well.

ADHD and Writing

Of all the primary academic tasks, typically the most difficult one for students with ADHD is written expression. In the earliest grades, the student with ADHD may be exceptionally slow in doing any written work. In the time it takes most other students to put the heading on their paper and copy the first three sentences from the board, the student with ADHD may still be working on getting his or her name and date in the heading. When writing tasks get more lengthy and complex in the higher grades, students with ADHD often report that they have many good ideas for what to write, but it takes them forever to put their thoughts into organized sentences and paragraphs.

Written expression makes more demands on the executive functions that are often impaired in ADHD than do reading and writing. The words and numbers found in texts and math problems provide a structure and an organization to assist the reader, whereas written expression requires students to organize, prioritize, sequence, and elaborate their thoughts in a structure they need to create. Slow processing speed is often characteristic of students with ADHD.

What Can Educators Do?

Assessment and diagnosis of ADHD usually require a licensed physician, psychologist, or other medical specialist who has been trained to recognize the disorder and design appropriate treatment. But classroom teachers and school administrators have an important role to play.

Educators who are aware of our new understandings about ADHD are better equipped to identify students who may be struggling with this disorder. When a student demonstrates impairments that may be related to ADHD, the teacher can describe the student's difficulties in detail and encourage the family to present this information to their pediatrician or other specialist. Such early identification can prevent students with ADHD from becoming demoralized by repeated experiences of frustration and failure and can ensure that they receive the assessment and support they need to succeed.

References

Biederman, J., Petty, C. R., Evans, M., Small, J., & Faraone, S. V. (2010). How persistent is ADHD? A controlled 10 year follow-up study of boys with ADHD. *Psychiatry Research 177*, 299–304.

Biederman, J., Petty, C. R., Monuteaux, M. C., Fried, R., Byrne, D., Mirto, T., Spencer, T., et al. (2010). Adult psychiatric outcomes of girls with attention-deficit hyperactivity disorder: 11-year follow-up in a longitudinal case-control study. *American Journal of Psychiatry. 167*(4), 409–417.

Faraone, S., Perlis, R. H., Doyle, A. E., Smoller, J. W., Goralnick, J. J., Holmgren, M. A. & Sklar, P. (2005). Molecular genetics of attention deficit/hyperactivity disorder. *Biological Psychiatry, 57*(11), 1313–1323.

Shaw, P., Eckstrand, K., Sharp, W., Blumenthal, J., Lerch, J. P., Greenstein, D., Clasen, L., et al. (2007). Attention-deficit/hyperactivity disorder is characterized by a delay in cortical maturation. *Proceedings of the National Academy of Sciences, 104*(49), 19649–19654.

Critical Thinking

1. What could you do as a teacher of young children to provide an environment that supports the learning of all children in your classroom?

2. Describe some strategies that are most effective to help children diagnosed with ADHD.

Internet References

ADHA Resource Center
  http://www.aacap.org/aacap/Families_and_Youth/Resource_Centers/ADHD_Resource_Center/Home.aspx
Child Mind Institute
  https://childmind.org/
National Resource on ADHD
  www.chadd.org
Trusted Guide to Mental and Emotional Health
  https://www.helpguide.org/

THOMAS E. BROWN is a clinical psychologist and associate director of the Yale Clinic for Attention and Related Disorders in New Haven, Connecticut.

Article   Prepared by: Karen Menke Paciorek, *Eastern Michigan University*

4 Disturbing Facts about Preschool Suspension

RASHEED MALIK

Learning Outcomes

After reading this article, you will be able to:

- Explain to others the increasing trend of preschool suspension and expulsion

- Describe why African American boys may be more likely to be suspended.

Several years ago, when Zakiya Sankara-Jabar's 3-year-old son was repeatedly suspended from preschool, she felt like a bad parent. "I started to think that there was something inherently wrong with my son," says Sankara-Jabar, who is now a parent advocate for race equity in schools. Her son was eventually expelled from his preschool, forcing Sankara-Jabar to drop out of college. While she now knows that their experience was likely due to implicit biases, it's little consolation. In a phone interview with the author, Sankara-Jabar recalled the ordeal as "a lot of toxic stress and trauma, not just for the children but even for the parents."

In the wake of pioneering research by Yale University's Walter Gilliam, the federal government started collecting data on public preschool suspension and expulsion in 2011. According to the most recent data from the U.S. Department of Education, 47 percent of the preschoolers who received suspensions or expulsions in the 2013–2014 school year were African American, even though they made up only 19 percent of preschool enrollment. In total, nearly 7,000 3- and 4-year-olds were suspended or expelled from public preschools during the same school year.

This column highlights four of the most important, and disturbing, facts to know about preschool suspension and expulsion.

1. It Pathologizes Normal Child Behavior

Children at the young ages of 3 or 4 often test boundaries and act out, particularly when adjusting to new social environments such as preschool. According to the American Academy of Pediatrics, it's perfectly normal for a preschooler's frustration or anger to manifest as physical conflict. When caregivers correct this ordinary behavior in a way that promotes empathy, it's a healthy part of a child's social development. Labeling a young child as violent or disruptive and calling parents to pick up their child sends the wrong message to the child, and it could even lead to unnecessary medical or psychological interventions.

In Sankara-Jabar's case that was the course that her son's preschool recommended. Although her son's tantrums were typical for his age, the preschool asked that he be evaluated in a medical setting. When she refused, she was told she would need to find another preschool for her son. Quite often, this is what preschool expulsion looks like.

In working with other parents on this issue, Sankara-Jabar says, "I have seen parents get bullied into medicating their children and signing them up for special needs classes. And this is more pronounced with African American boys." Yet in 2014, an Indiana University analysis of the literature on racial differences in child behavior showed that children of color and White children act out at the same rates.

2. It Can Be Driven by Implicit Racial Bias

Last year, in a study that used sophisticated eye-tracking technology, Yale researchers led by Gilliam found that preschool teachers tend to more closely observe African American children than White children when they are expecting challenging behavior. The researchers believe that this could help explain the disproportionate levels of discipline experienced by African American boys, who represent 19 percent of male enrollment but receive 45 percent of male suspensions.

Researchers describe this error in judgment as implicit bias, and it can be observed in preschool teachers of all races. In fact, the study found that African American teachers held African American students to a higher standard of behavior than White teachers. As an advocate, Sankara-Jabar has noticed this bias, saying, "It's almost like people have sort of been socialized that African Americans, and African American males in particular, are just inherently bad. Like they're born bad."

3. It's More Common in School Districts That Still Use Corporal Punishment*

The new CAP analysis also finds that in the same school year, schools that reported using corporal punishment as a disciplinary tactic suspended or expelled preschoolers at twice the rate of schools that did not use corporal punishment. To be clear, these schools are not necessarily using corporal punishment in their preschool classrooms. Nonetheless, this finding reflects an institutional reliance on harsh discipline rather than the more effective practice of redirecting disruptive behavior. When teachers are given the supports and the right tools to help children with challenging behavior, they can lower rates of hyperactivity, restlessness, and externalizing behaviors.

4. It May Be an Even Bigger Problem in Private Preschools

The only recent data available on preschool discipline comes from public schools. But as in Sankara-Jabar's case, it is likely that most instances of suspension and expulsion happen in private preschools. In her experience, Sankara-Jabar notes that "this becomes a child care nightmare for parents because their kids are constantly being kicked out of these private preschools." The only study that has collected data on disciplinary rates in private preschools found that in 2005, the rates of expulsion in private preschools were twice as high as those seen in public preschools.

Without accountability and reliable data reporting, private preschools remain free to discriminate against families of color.

Conclusion

In recent years, the positive effects of high-quality preschool have been repeatedly documented. As more cities and states attempt to provide public preschool, strong civil rights protections must be in place to ensure that the destructive practice of preschool suspension does not become more widespread. Meanwhile, the Department of Education's Office for Civil Rights, the office responsible for collecting data on the practice in public schools, has been targeted by the Trump administration for downsizing. Furthermore, researchers have yet to fully diagnose the scope of the problem in private preschool settings.

The good news is that with the right training and professional supports for preschool teachers, the normal yet challenging behaviors of 3- and 4-year-olds can be redirected in positive ways that help them develop the social and emotional skills necessary for learning. Armed with the new cutting-edge research on implicit bias in preschools, many early educators are working hard to end the practices of suspension and expulsion. After all, preschool should be a welcoming place where children grow and develop normally, free from society's stereotypes and prejudice.

Critical Thinking

1. Choose one of the four facts provided in the article and reflect on what you may have observed that would apply to that fact regarding preschool suspension.

2. How could racial bias affect preschool suspension or expulsion?

Internet References

Preschool Expulsion: A Child's Perspective
https://www.zerotothree.org/resources/132-preschool-expulsion-a-child-s-perspective

Reducing Suspension and Expulsion Practices in Early Childhood Settings
https://www.acf.hhs.gov/ecd/child-health-development/reducing-suspension-and-expulsion-practices

Standing Together against Suspension and Expulsion in Early Childhood Education
http://www.naeyc.org/blogs/suspension-expulsion-early-childhood

RASHEED MALIK is a policy analyst for the Early Childhood Policy team at the Center for American Progress.

*Note: Author's calculations using the U.S. Department of Education's 2013–2014 Civil Rights Data Collection.

Article   Prepared by: Karen Menke Paciorek, *Eastern Michigan University*

Teach Up for Excellence

All students deserve equitable access to an engaging and rigorous curriculum.

CAROL ANN TOMLINSON AND EDWIN LOU JAVIUS

Learning Outcomes

After reading this article, you will be able to:

- Choose one of the principles of teaching up the authors describe in the article and describe how that would look if implemented in your future classroom.

- Describe what the authors call "peacock" moments of success.

Within the lifetime of a significant segment of the population, schools in the United States operated under the banner of "separate but equal" opportunity. In time, and at considerable cost, we came to grips with the reality that separate is seldom equal. But half a century later, and with integration a given, many of our students still have separate and drastically unequal learning experiences (Darling-Hammond, 2010).

Many of our schools are overwhelmingly attended by low-income and racially and linguistically diverse students, whereas nearby schools are largely attended by students from more affluent and privileged backgrounds (Kozol, 2005). Another kind of separateness exists *within* schools. It's frequently the case that students attend classes that correlate highly with learners' race and socioeconomic status, with less privileged students in lower learning groups or tracks and more privileged students in more advanced ones (Darling-Hammond, 2010).

The logic behind separating students by what educators perceive to be their ability is that it enables teachers to provide students with the kind of instruction they need. Teachers can remediate students who perform at a lower level of proficiency and accelerate those who perform at a higher level. All too often, however, students in lower-level classrooms receive a level of education that ensures they will remain at the tail end

of the learning spectrum. High-end students may (or may not) experience rich and challenging learning opportunities, and students in the middle too often encounter uninspired learning experiences that may not be crippling but are seldom energizing. No group comes to know, understand, and value the others. Schools in which this arrangement is the norm often display an "us versus them" attitude that either defines the school environment or dwells just below the surface of daily exchanges.

Difficult to Defend

Research finds that sorting, this 21st century version of school segregation, correlates strongly with student race and economic status and predicts and contributes to student outcomes, with students in higher-level classes typically experiencing better teachers, curriculum, and achievement levels than peers in lower-level classes (Carbonaro & Gamoran, 2003). Further, when lower-performing students experience curriculum and instruction focused on meaning and understanding, they increase their skills at least as much as their higher-achieving peers do (Educational Research Service, 1992).

These findings are even more problematic when combined with our current understanding that the human brain is incredibly malleable and that individuals can nearly always outperform our expectations for them. The sorting mechanisms often used in school are not only poor predictors of success in life, but also poor measures of what a young person can accomplish, given the right context (Dweck, 2007). Virtually all students would benefit from the kind of curriculum and instruction we have often reserved for advanced learners—that is, curriculum and instruction designed to engage students, with a focus on meaning making, problem solving, logical thinking, and transfer of learning (National Research Council, 1999).

In addition, the demographic reality is that low-income students of color and English language learners will soon become

Response to Intervention and Early Childhood Best Practices: Working Hand in Hand So All Children Can Learn by Karen Wise Lindeman

93

> **RTI is a systematic and intentional framework for ensuring all children learn. When combined with early childhood best practices, it has the potential to increase children's learning and catch delays early.**

Also, teachers can use several different levels of interventions for different domains. A child can receive Tier 2 interventions for an academic skill and Tier 3 interventions for behavior (Greenwood et al. 2011). For example, Luke is making progress with the teacher's small group (Tier 2) literacy interventions but still needs direct, intense, one-on-one (Tier 3) interventions to help control his strong emotional reactions when taking turns with other children. If he does not make progress with Tier 3 interventions, the team can decide if a full evaluation is necessary. RTI is not the only path to special education services (McCabe 2006; CRTIEC 2009), and RTI should not delay a child from receiving such services.

So tell Kurt's school district about the accommodations you have already tried with the struggling preschooler— show them your portfolios, checklists, observations, and progress-monitoring results—and continue to keep his parents and other professionals involved in the discussion, as needed. Early childhood best practices require educators to *respond to* young children and provide high-quality, developmentally appropriate *interventions*.

Conclusion

RTI is a systematic and intentional framework for ensuring all children learn. When combined with early childhood best practices, RTI has the potential to increase children's learning and catch delays early. Each tier allows teachers to respond in developmentally appropriate ways to young children, in partnership with families and other professionals. Educators need to be empowered to develop quality early childhood practices at each tier. RTI can improve intentional and explicit early interventions and help to meet individual children's needs. If a child does not respond to these interventions, preschool teachers, other professionals, and families can problem solve strategies to ensure success. RTI and early childhood best practices can go hand in hand so all children can learn.

References

Barnett, D.W., A.M. VanDerHeyden, & J.C. Witt. 2007. "Achieving Science-Based Practice Through Response to Intervention: What It Might Look Like in Preschools." *Journal of Educational and Psychological Consultation* 17(1): 31–54.

Barton, R., & J. Stepanek. 2009. "Three Tiers to Success." *Principal Leadership* 9(8): 16–20.

Callender, W.A. 2012. "Why Principals Should Adopt Schoolwide RTI." *Principal* 91(4): 8–12.

Coleman, M.R., V. Buysse, & J. Neitzel. 2006. *Recognition and Response: An Early Intervening System for Young Children At-Risk for Learning Disabilities.* Chapel Hill: The University of North Carolina at Chapel Hill, FPG Child Development Institute. www.readingrockets.org/article/11394/.

Coleman, M.R., F.P. Roth, & T. West. 2009. *Roadmap to Pre-K RtI: Applying Response to Intervention in Preschool Settings.* New York: The National Center for Learning Disabilities. www.sde.idaho.gov/site/rti/resourcesDocs/Early%20Childhood/roadmaptoprekrti.pdf.

Copple, C., & S. Bredekamp, eds. 2009. *Developmentally Appropriate Practice in Early Childhood Programs: Serving Children From Birth Through Age 8.* 3rd ed. Washington, DC: NAEYC.

CRTIEC (Center for Response to Intervention in Early Childhood). 2009. "Myths About Response to Intervention in Early Childhood." www.cde.state.co.us/early/downloads/CFCoorMtgs/Multi%20Tier%20System/MythsaboutRtIinEarlyChildhood-Final9-1-09.pdf.

DEC (Division for Early Childhood of the Council for Exceptional Children), NAEYC, & NHSA (National Head Start Association). 2013. "Frameworks for Response to Intervention in Early Childhood: Description and Implications." Arlington, VA: DEC; Washington, DC: NAEYC; Alexandria, VA: NHSA. www.naeyc.org/content/frameworks-response-intervention.

Elliott, J. 2008. "Response to Intervention: What & Why?" *The School Administrator* 65(8): 10–18. www.aasa.org/SchoolAdministratorArticle.aspx?id=4932.

Greenwood, C.R., T. Bradfield, R. Kaminski, M. Linas, J.J. Carta, & D. Nylander. 2011. "The Response to Intervention (RTI) Approach in Early Childhood." *Focus on Exceptional Children* 43(9): 1–22. www.milcleaders.org/media/cms/files/Content/Pages/Focus%20on%20Exceptional%20Children.pdf.

McCabe, P.C. 2006. "Responsiveness to Intervention (RTI) in Early Childhood: Challenges and Practical Guidelines." *Journal of Early Childhood and Infant Psychology* 2: 157–180.

NCLB (No Child Left Behind Act of 2001). Pub. L. No. 107–110, 115 Stat. 1425.

Walker-Dalhouse, D., & V.J. Risko. 2009. "Crossing Boundaries and Initiating Conversations About RTI: Understanding and Applying Differentiated Classroom Instruction." *The Reading Teacher* 63(1): 84–87.

Critical Thinking

1. Why are families an integral part of the team, especially when it comes to Tier 3 interventions?

2. Explain how intentional teaching and RTI work together to provide optimal learning experiences for all children.

Internet References

The Council for Exceptional Children (CEC)
www.cec.sped.org

Intervention Central
www.interventioncentral.org

National Center on Response to Intervention
www.rti4success.org

National Association for the Education of Young Children
www.naeyc.org

National School Boards Association
www.nsba.org

KAREN WISE LINDEMAN, PhD, is an assistant professor and early childhood program coordinator at State University of New York (SUNY) at Fredonia. Karen's past roles include prekindergarten and kindergarten teacher, early intervention service provider, and teacher of the deaf. karen.lindeman@fredonia.edu.

Unit 5

UNIT

Prepared by: Karen Menke Paciorek, *Eastern Michigan University*

Practices that Help Children Thrive in School

There is such discord going on in our profession when it comes to play, a core principle of our field. Early Childhood researchers, professionals, and teachers speak constantly about the need for children to engage in freely chosen exploration and manipulation of a variety of materials, yet giving children the opportunity to do so often results in criticism from administrators who are focused on raising test scores. It is similar to the volumes of research on the importance of eating a healthy diet and exercising as obesity is our major health issue. We read the research but choose to follow another path. It's time for early childhood educators to arm themselves with the data to speak with conviction about the need for children to interact with materials that engage their minds and cause them to ponder, think, create, and explore. This is not an either or debate looking at academics vs. play. Engaging in new learning experiences should be in a rich environment that does contain content teachers share with children. It also needs to offer time for the children to explore and think about the content they are learning and make connections through hands on discovery experiences. Early childhood educators need to do a more thorough job of documenting the learning occurring in their classrooms and explain to others the early learning standards being acquired and how the children are applying their learning. With some more public relations (PR) work, we will be successful in educating others about the best ways children learn and yes, play and exploration is one of the key ways. Anyone who watches television can recall the many advertisements for prescription drugs. Those commercials always include the tag line, "side effects may include . . ." We need to do a better job of publicizing the side effects of play. Sharing with families, "The side effects of play will include increased curiosity, problem solving, communication, fine motor development, cognitive skills and many other positive effects." Let's all put on our PR hat and be more proactive in our message instead of being reactive by responding to yet another complaint from a parent that all their child does is play in your classroom.

Recently, I conducted a professional development in-service session for all of the kindergarten and first grade teachers in a school district located in the suburbs of a large Midwest city. The one issue about which the teachers were most concerned was the lack of time for play for their children. The administration even went so far as to cancel recess and required teachers to have a detailed lesson plan if children were to be away from their desks for more than five minutes. The articles in this unit serve as resources for any staff looking for research that supports the need for play in programs and schools serving children in the early childhood years. The development of important social and emotional skills during the early childhood years will serve the children well as they move through childhood and into adulthood. Social and emotional skills are best learned in natural settings where children have to rely on skills they have previously developed as they navigate the challenge of making friends, figuring out how they fit in to society and begin to develop an idea of how others see them as an individual.

Continuing the discussion on play, educators receive many questions from parents about what is called rough and tumble or big body play among young children. The need for children to engage in appropriate large muscle play is strong and the development of gross motor skills and the ability to control those muscles is a valuable skill to learn. As educators, we constantly straddle that line between what is developmentally appropriate for children's development and legal restrictions placed on educators from school administrators and insurance companies. A balance can be found and there is no need to eliminate playgrounds or recess for legal issues if there is proper supervision and appropriate and well-maintained equipment. Many insurance companies serving educational institutions have developed outstanding resource materials which provide appropriate guidelines.

When planning your classroom activities, make sure that action is a part of the class pace. The children should be actively questioning and investigating, while the teachers are supporting the exploration and discussions. Children who approach learning with wonder and aww are those who will spend their life seeking answers and looking for solutions to problems. These traits can be introduced and fostered during the early childhood years. Teachers can plan effectively by purposefully providing materials, activities, and opportunities for students to come to know and truly understand their learning. If teachers understand how young children learn, they can be successful in engaging their students in developmentally appropriate activities and in avoiding the risks of early academic instruction.

Another practice that is increasing in its trend is academic redshirting, named after the practice of a college athlete sitting out a year to develop and grow stronger. This practice involves the parents not enrolling children in kindergarten when they are age eligible to attend. Parents are interested in having their children be the most academically ready for school and the oldest in the class. However, this practice has some potential long-term costs. Educators and economists are weary of parents holding their children back and not considering all of the ramifications of this practice that involves 11 percent of children. Early childhood organizations have all recommended that children start kindergarten when they are age eligible. The responsibility to be ready to start school does not belong to the student, for it is the school and teachers' responsibility to meet the educational needs of each child.

When discussing educational practices, the idea of rushing or pushing is an uninvited pressure that has crept into the policies and decisions made for young children. Children born today have an excellent chance of living long lives into their 90s. There is no need to rush and acquire skills that can easily be learned after the child has built a strong foundation of exploration and discovery, especially at the expense of valuable lifetime lessons that are learned best when children are young. Preschoolers and kindergartners need to learn lifelong social skills such as getting along with others, making wise choices, negotiating, developing compassion and empathy, and communicating needs, to name a few. The basics are a solid foundation to understanding how things work, the exploration and manipulation of materials, and the many opportunities for creative expressions. A walk down any toy store aisle by someone not familiar with toys on the market today will be the foundation for a rich discussion on the new materials available and their effects on young children.

Creativity is one word often associated with teachers and many envy the opportunities for engaging in creative endeavors effective teachers provide for their students. Early childhood educators must continue to provide a variety of opportunities for children to explore, create, and problem solve using a variety of materials. Many of the key issues facing our society will be solved by creative solutions only developed after much exploration. I currently see a growing number of teachers gathering baskets of loose parts for children to use in a variety of ways in their play. Children can be creative with a variety of materials they can move around more than when given fixed items that can only be used one way. This especially applies out on the playground where a collection of boards, spools, and tubes offers many more opportunities for collaboration than one set in place climber.

We know that teachers possess and exert significant power and control over what occurs in their classrooms. That is a huge responsibility, and teachers should receive all of the support necessary to enable them to carry through with the many requirements of the job. The influence teachers have over the students in their classrooms has a strong impact even with the influx of technology and media sources. We need to give teachers the strategies and skills to lead with the understanding of what is best for children and what will encourage the students' development and learning. I get frustrated when I visit schools and am in classrooms in which I would not want to spend one hour, let along three to eleven hours some young children spend in formal education settings each and every day. I see classrooms with all life and joy sucked right out of them and instead occupied by children void of energy or excitement for learning. If zest and passion for teaching is not part of what you bring to your job each and every day, then consider another profession. Children's successes depend on highly motivated and skilled teachers who understand the importance of what they do. As Abraham Lincoln said, "Whatever you are, be a good one."

It is my hope this unit will encourage teachers to hone their skills and strategies. Teachers, you have the power. You have the power to inspire, encourage, and teach. Use your power wisely. Be a thoughtful, intentional educator as you work to understand practices, implement them, and provide optimal opportunities for young children to thrive under your care. Read these articles with the promise that you will use your power for the good. Read these articles with the goal to reflect on your practice and improve on your skills. The students want to thrive in their learning, but will you help them?

Article   Prepared by: Karen Menke Paciorek, *Eastern Michigan University*

Quality 101: Identifying the Core Components of a High-quality Early Childhood Program

SIMON WORKMAN AND REBECCA ULLRICH

Learning Outcomes

After reading this article, you will be able to:

- Advocate for every child having access to quality early childhood education.

- Identify skills a quality leader will possess to create and foster a high-quality and developmentally appropriate learning environment.

Every day, millions of American families go through a familiar ritual: dropping off their young child at childcare or preschool. And while there are many reasons why parents choose a particular program—cost, location, the teachers, shared values, and the program's specific focus—one thing is universal: As parents walk away from the classroom in the morning to start their own day, each of them hopes that they have made the right decision and that their child will have a rich and fulfilling day, supported by a loving and affectionate caregiver.

Unfortunately, parents often have very few childcare options and limited ways to really know the quality of care their child is receiving. The level to which basic needs are met—keeping the child well fed, safe, and clean—is usually easy to verify, but determining if one's child is engaging sufficiently and is participating in age-appropriate learning activities is much harder to ascertain.

The need for high-quality early childhood education has never been greater. Increasingly, children are growing up in families where all available parents are working—out of

necessity as well as choice. Furthermore, research continues to affirm the short- and long-term benefits for children who participate in high-quality early learning programs.[1] However, parents face significant barriers when searching for high-quality care. Waitlists are long and employers are inflexible, high-quality programs are expensive, and parents often lack the necessary tools to evaluate program quality. Many families live in childcare "deserts," and even when programs are available, quality is not well-regulated or supported by local, state, or federal policies, putting it out of reach for most families.[2]

This childcare crisis has received increased attention in recent years, from policy makers, political candidates, and voters.[3] However, there remains a critical need to better understand the components of high-quality programs to ensure policy solutions adequately support and promote access to quality for all families. To that end, this issue briefly highlights three core indicators of high-quality early childhood programs and identifies six structural supports that are necessary to achieve and maintain high quality. These indicators and supports provide a roadmap for policy makers as they develop solutions to the current childcare crisis and can also serve as a guide for parents seeking to make the best and most informed choices for their child.

Why Does Quality Matter?

A large body of research has demonstrated the critical importance of the first three years of a child's life.[4] The experiences and interactions children have in these early years significantly affects brain development and helps to establish the foundation for future learning.[5] Warm and responsive interactions can create a nurturing and stable environment that enables the development of secure attachments between children and their caregivers—both those within and beyond their families. These attachments support children as they develop a sense of self and begin to understand their emotions, and they lay the foundation for establishing successful relationships at later ages.[6] With an estimated 6 million young children enrolled in childcare, it is clear that early learning programs, and the people who work in them, have a critical role to play in child development—a role that complements parents.[7] Furthermore, this crucial development must be supported from infancy, when brain development is at its peak. Waiting until children enter preschool or kindergarten to introduce these vital interventions is simply too late.

The positive effects of high-quality early childhood programs on specific, short- and long-term outcomes for children, families, and communities, have been quantified by numerous research studies.[8] In the short to medium term, children enrolled in high-quality early learning programs are less likely to need special education services during their K-12 years, are less likely to commit juvenile offenses, and more likely to graduate from high school. In the long term, those participating children are more likely to be employed and less likely to be dependent on government assistance.[9] The positive effects are larger, and more likely to be sustained, when programs are high quality.[10] In addition, the impact is greatest for children from low-income families.[11] Differences in children's cognitive abilities by income are evident at only nine months old and significantly widen by the time children are two years old.[12] Children living in poverty are more likely to be subject to stressful home environments—which can have lifelong impacts on learning, cognition, and self-regulation—while parents living in poverty have limited resources to provide for their families and high barriers to access affordable, high-quality childcare.[13] High-quality early learning programs staffed by warm and responsive adults can help mitigate these effects, offering a safe and predictable learning environment that fosters children's development.[14]

Despite evidence of the positive impact of high-quality early childhood education for all children, it remains out of reach for most low- and moderate-income families.[15] The average price of center-based care in the United States accounts for nearly 30 percent of the median family income, and only 10 percent of childcare programs are considered high quality.[16] Publicly funded programs—such as Head Start, Early Head Start, childcare, and state pre-K programs—are primarily targeted at low-income families, but limited funding for these programs severely hinders access.[17] This lack of access to high-quality early childhood education perpetuates the achievement gap, evidenced by the fact that only 48 percent of low-income children are ready for kindergarten, compared with 75 percent of moderate- or high-income children.[18]

Moderate-income families are typically ineligible for these publicly funded programs, but at the same time, such families struggle to afford the high cost of care in the private sector.[19] This leaves parents facing a series of difficult choices, including prioritizing childcare expenses over other household necessities; settling for low-quality childcare that fits their budget; patching together multiple informal care options; or leaving the workforce altogether.[20] To ensure that all children can realize the gains that come from attending high-quality early childhood programs, policy solutions need to focus on improving program supports and creating funding strategies that will increase access to high-quality programs for children from all backgrounds.

What Does High Quality Look Like?

All states have regulations or licensing standards that childcare providers must meet in order to legally operate in the state. These regulations provide a baseline standard and are primarily focused on protecting children from harm rather than on advancing child development and early learning.[21] While these standards are critically important to children's well-being—mitigating risks from inadequate supervision, poor building and hygiene standards, and unsafe practices—they do not address the comprehensive needs of young children. As such, meeting licensing requirements serves only as a baseline providing the fundamental components necessary for operation rather than an indication of program quality. In addition, states have varying requirements when it comes to determining exactly which providers need to be licensed, often making exemptions for faith-based programs or based on the number of nonrelative children served. As a result, significant numbers of children attend license-exempt programs that are not required to meet even the minimum licensing standard.[22]

Moreover, the key to a high-quality program is what happens inside the classroom or family childcare home, namely the interactions that take place between the teacher and child.[23] In a high-quality program, teachers engage children with learning strategies that are tailored to the age of the child and use an appropriate curriculum to structure the learning experience.[24] A variety of supports are needed to facilitate these interactions so that high-quality teaching and learning can occur. As such, the quality of an early childhood program is dependent on the following three key factors.

Interpersonal Interactions

The learning environment created by a teacher is critical to the quality of an early childhood program.[25] The experiences that a child has in their earliest years shape their development, and teachers play an important role in creating those experiences. A well-trained and highly skilled teacher tailors their interactions to fit the needs of the child—using responsive language, engaging all children in classroom activities, fostering independence, and creating a language-rich environment.[26] Effective early childhood teachers proactively prevent and redirect challenging behavior and respond to children's needs with respect, warmth, and empathy. The experiences children have with teachers in their earliest years can also set the tone for their interactions with teachers in later grades and thus are crucial to promoting positive attitudes about school and approaches to learning.[27]

Physical Environment

Children need a physical setting—both inside and outdoors—where they can play, explore, and learn safely. The learning environment needs to include engaging and developmentally appropriate materials and be arranged to promote independence and exploration based on children's different stages of development. For example, infants need to interact with their environment in a very physical way, examining cause and effect relationships by touching and feeling objects. The environment should therefore include toys made of different materials that are small enough to be picked up by an infant.

Toddlers and preschoolers use objects in more complex combinations and engage in sociodramatic play with one another. Their environment needs toys that spark the imagination, such as play kitchens, and that can engage them in problem solving such as puzzles.[28] Learning centers—clearly defined areas set aside in a learning environment where children can have easy access to materials and engage in independent and self-directed learning activities—can be an effective way to organize and support developing abilities, encourage interactions, create opportunities for role playing, and promote literacy skills.[29]

In addition to the indoor learning environment, children need access to outdoor space where they can move and engage with the natural world. Outdoor play has positive impacts on health and has been shown to combat childhood obesity and help develop stronger immune systems.[30] Research also shows that children who play outdoors regularly have more active imaginations, lower stress levels, and have greater respect for themselves and others.[31]

Program Support Structure

A high-functioning operating environment is an essential element of a quality early childhood program. This administrative operational support takes a number of forms. First, programs need effective leaders who can provide instructional support to teachers as well as sound business management to the overall program.[32] These multiple leadership functions are complex and often need to be fulfilled by more than one person. Second, external to the immediate program, programs need a series of structural supports, including access to professional development, quality improvement resources, stable and sufficient funding streams, and a pipeline of well-trained teachers. These external supports recognize that early childhood programs do not operate in a vacuum and rely on the wider early childhood system.[33]

All three factors need to be in place to ensure quality. A well-resourced classroom is not sufficient without an effective teacher to harness those resources. Meanwhile, an effective teacher is not sustainable without a support system to manage the business, support instruction, and provide professional development.

How States Measure Quality in Early Childhood

While there is no single definition of high quality and therefore no single measurement tool to determine and compare early childhood program quality across the United States, there are a number of tools that are widely used to assess and report the quality of early childhood programs.

Environment rating scales: The Early Childhood Environment Rating Scale, or ECERS for children ages 3–5, the Infant/Toddler Environment Rating Scale, and the Family Child Care Environment Rating Scale are standardized tools used to measure process quality at the classroom level. The measures contain multiple items on which programs are rated, organized into seven subscales. These subscales include ratings of the space and furnishing, personal care routines, the activities and interactions that take place in the classroom, and how the program engages with families. Ultimately, these tools are designed to assess the various interactions that occur in the learning environment—for example, between staff and children and among children themselves, the interactions children have with materials and activities, and the structures that support these interactions such as the space and the schedule.[34]

CLASS: The Classroom Assessment Scoring System, or CLASS, is an observation tool that assesses the interactions between teachers and children that affect learning and development. CLASS has separate scales for different age groups, reflecting the differences in how infants, toddlers, and preschoolers learn. The infant observation has just one domain while the pre-K observation has three domains. The observation assesses the quality of relationships, routines, the organization of the physical environment, and the way language is used, and interactions are facilitated to prompt children to think critically.[35]

intentionally. This article summarizes research on the development of preschool children's critical thinking skills and suggests practical, research-based strategies for supporting them.

Reasoning and Problem-Solving Skills

Definitions of critical thinking skills vary, although nearly all include reasoning, making judgments and conclusions, and solving problems (Willingham 2008; Lai 2011). Although it was previously believed that these were higher-order thinking skills that developed only in older children and adults (Piaget 1930), research demonstrates that children reason and problem solve as early as infancy (e.g., Woodward 2009). Between ages 3 and 5 children form complex thoughts and insights, and during the preschool years their cognitive abilities—including logical thinking and reasoning—develop substantially (Amsterlaw & Wellman 2006). These skills enable children to recognize, understand, and analyze a problem and draw on knowledge or experience to seek solutions to the problem (USDHHS 2010). Some researchers conclude that reasoning and problem-solving skills are domain specific (e.g., reasoning skills in science do not necessarily transfer to mathematics); others, however, argue that teachers can foster young children's general critical thinking skills (see Lai 2011 for a review).

Reasoning and problem-solving skills are foundational for lifelong learning. Analyzing arguments, making inferences, reasoning, and implementing decisions to solve problems are important skills across all content areas and thus critical for school success. The ability to efficiently gather, understand, analyze, and interpret information is increasingly necessary to function in school and in the workplace (Schneider 2002). Educators and policy makers, now more than ever, recognize the need to foster critical thinking skills in young children. This is evidenced in the Common Core State Standards, which emphasize the importance of reasoning and problem-solving skills in preparing children for "college, workforce training, and life in a technological society" (NGA Center & CCSSO 2010, 4).

Key Ideas about Children's Thinking

Three key ideas emerge from the research on young children's thinking:

1. Young children are capable of developing reasoning and problem-solving skills.
2. Children's early reasoning and problem-solving skills support their later development and learning.
3. Early childhood educators can foster children's reasoning and problem solving.

Research suggests how these ideas relate to everyday practice.

Young Children Can Develop Reasoning and Problem-Solving Skills

Scholars long believed that true logical reasoning does not develop until adolescence (Piaget 1930). However, recent research suggests that logical thinking and reasoning begin in infancy and develop gradually throughout childhood (Gopnik et al. 2004; Hollister Sandberg & McCullough 2010). From infancy on, children pay attention to people's intentions and goals, and infants as young as 6 months old demonstrate rudimentary reasoning skills (Woodward 2009).

Early reasoning skills. Woodward and her colleagues explored how infants make sense of their physical and social worlds and develop reasoning skills (e.g., Hamlin, Hallinan, & Woodward 2008; Cannon & Woodward 2012). The researchers tested whether 7-month-olds would copy an experimenter's actions if they understood the experimenter's intention (Hamlin, Hallinan, & Woodward 2008). Infants were shown two toys, and then they watched as the experimenter reached for one of the toys and grasped it. The experimenter pushed the toys within reach of the infants and said, "Now it's your turn!" Infants reliably touched the same object the experimenter had grasped. This was not the case when the experimenter simply brushed the toy with the back of her hand rather than grasped it (suggesting that the touch was unintentional, not goal directed). In both cases the experimenter's actions drew attention to the object, but infants responded only when they interpreted the experimenter's actions as goal directed. These results, along with others from a series of studies Woodward and colleagues conducted, demonstrate that infants as young as 7 months old can analyze others' intentions and use this information to reason about things in their world (Woodward 2009).

Understanding of causality. Between 9 and 12 months, infants begin to understand that one event or behavior causes another (Woodward 2009), and 2-year-olds are adept at using causality in their thinking (McMullen 2013). Gopnik and colleagues (2000; 2001) designed a series of experiments to explore how young children construct and test explanations for events. They showed children a "magical" light box that glowed when it was activated. Although the experimenter controlled the box, the box appeared to be activated by placing a block on top of it. The experimenter showed 2- to 4-year-old children different blocks, some that turned the box on (the experimenter called these *blickets*) and some that did not (not blickets). The children were asked which block was the blicket. Children as young as 2 were able to draw causal conclusions about which object was the blicket, correctly choosing the block that had "activated" the light. In another experiment with 3- and 4-year-old children, the task was modified so two blocks were placed on the machine and children were asked which block to remove to make the machine stop lighting up. Children correctly predicted which object they should remove from the box to make it stop.

The blicket studies are important because they demonstrate that very young children understand how one thing affects another and that as children get older, their reasoning skills are more sophisticated. Children are increasingly able to generate theories about the causal effects of objects and to test those theories by asking questions and making predictions.

Inductive and deductive reasoning. Understanding cause and effect is an important component of both inductive and deductive reasoning, which develop between the ages of 3 and 6 (Schraw et al. 2011). Young children use *inductive reasoning* when they generalize the conclusions they draw from the consequences of their own behaviors or experiences. *Deductive reasoning* is the process by which individuals use facts or general rules to draw a conclusion, being able to understand the premise "If *P* happens, then *Q* will too" (Schraw et al. 2011).

Three-year-old Maya has a fireplace at home and has learned through experience that fires are hot and should not be touched. When she sees the flame on a gas stove in the kitchen at her early childhood program, she reasons that the stove is also hot and should not be touched. "Hot," she says to her friend. "Don't touch!" Maya uses inductive reasoning in this situation, generalizing and extending her knowledge about fire and heat to a new situation.

> **Although young children's deductive reasoning becomes more sophisticated with age, their development of this reasoning is complex.**

Three-year-old Brandon knows that if it is nighttime, it is time for him to take a bath (if *P*, then *Q*). Through repeated experiences—nighttime (P), then bath (Q)—Brandon connects these two events using deductive reasoning, the basis for making predictions. Inductive and deductive reasoning skills grow substantially during the preschool years as a result of children's increasing knowledge and varied experiences and interactions with the world around them.

Analogical reasoning. Goswami and Pauen (2005) have spent many years researching how *analogical reasoning,* a form of inductive reasoning that involves making and understanding comparisons, develops in young children (Goswami 1995; Goswami & Pauen 2005). In a series of three experiments, they tested the ability of 3- and 4-year-olds to make comparisons, or relational mappings, based on size (Goswami 1995). An experimenter read *Goldilocks and the Three Bears* to a child, and then said they were going to play a game about choosing cups. The experimenter said, "We are each going to have a set of cups, a daddy-bear-size cup, a mummy-bear-size

cup, and a baby-bear-size cup, and you have to choose the same cup from your set that I choose from mine." The experimenter named the cups in her set (e.g., "I'm choosing the Mummy cup") but not in the child's set. To choose the correct cup, the child had to work out the size relationship between the two sets of cups using one-to-one correspondence. Not only did 3- and 4-year-old children choose the correct cup, they could do so even when the positions and colors of their cups were different from those of the experimenter's cups.

However, when experimenters asked 3- and 4-year-olds to make analogies (comparisons) involving concepts rather than physical characteristics (e.g., A is hotter than B is hotter than C, or A is louder than B is louder than C), only the 4-year-olds were successful (Goswami 1995; Goswami & Pauen 2005). Goswami concluded that children as young as 3 can use analogies as a basis for reasoning only if the analogy is based on a familiar structure, such as the characters in *Goldilocks*. This skill develops and becomes more sophisticated over time, doing so rather rapidly during the brief time between ages 3 and 4.

Reasoning with abstract ideas. Research demonstrates that although young children's deductive reasoning becomes more sophisticated with age and that 4-year-olds can reason using abstract ideas, their development of this reasoning is complex. For example, a teacher is working with a small group of children. She says, "We're going to think about some silly stories together. Some of the stories may sound funny, but I want you to think carefully about them. For each story, I'm going to ask you to use your imagination and make a picture in your head. In this story, all cats bark. So the cats that are in your head, are they barking? Are they meowing? Now, Jeremy is a cat. Is Jeremy barking? Is Jeremy meowing? How do you know?" Problems like this actually get more difficult for children as they get older and acquire more real-world experience, because they are more likely to know of counterexamples ("I know a cat that can't 'meow'!"). However, children eventually overcome this and draw the correct conclusions from complex, even absurd, premises (Hollister Sandburg & McCullough 2010).

Children's Early Reasoning and Problem-Solving Skills Support Their Later Development and Learning

Cognitive learning. Children's reasoning and problem-solving skills are associated with a range of important literacy learning (e.g., Tzuriel & Flor-Maduel 2010) and mathematics outcomes (Grissmer et al. 2010). In an analysis of six longitudinal data sets, researchers found that general knowledge at kindergarten entry was the strongest predictor of children's science and reading skills and a strong predictor of math skills (Grissmer et al. 2010). General knowledge includes children's thinking and reasoning skills, in particular their ability to form questions about the natural world, gather evidence, and communicate conclusions (USDOE 2002).

Social-emotional learning. Children's reasoning and problem-solving skills are also important components of social and emotional competence. Social problem-solving skills include generating a number of alternative solutions to a conflict and understanding and considering the consequences of one's behaviors (Denham & Almeida 1987; Denham et al. 2012). These skills are linked to children's long-term behavioral outcomes (Youngstrom et al. 2000), school adjustment (Bierman et al. 2008), and academic success (Greenberg, Kusché, & Riggs 2001).

To see how reasoning and problem solving apply to the social-emotional domain, let's return to Sandy's classroom a couple of months after Keira's first experience with creating an experiment to test a hypothesis:

Keira notices Andy and Eric creating a zoo with animals and blocks in the block area and asks, "Can I play with you?" Andy responds, "No, there's not enough animals for three people!" Upset, Keira says to her teacher, Sandy, "Andy won't play with me because I'm a girl." Sandy bends down to Keira's eye level and says, "Are you sure? I saw you and Andy playing together just this morning on the playground. Can you think of any other reasons Andy might not want to play with you right now?" Keira says, "Well, maybe because there aren't enough animals for me too." Sandy asks Keira where she might find some other animals to add to the zoo. Keira finds several animal puppets in the book area and takes them to the block area.

As this situation demonstrates, children's daily experiences offer opportunities to construct explanations about cause and effect. When teachers provide enriching experiences and materials and support children's interactions with each other, they enable children to develop their reasoning.

In addition to these general teaching practices, there are specific strategies that promote preschool children's reasoning and problem-solving skills. These strategies, described in detail in the following three sections, promote "thoughtful decision

Checklist of Teaching Practices and Strategies to Support Preschool Children's Problem Solving and Reasoning

- **Facilitate children's play.** Support children's exploratory play experiences by providing challenging, varied materials that appeal to all of the senses—sight, sound, smell, touch, and taste. Encourage communication during play by extending children's language with their peers and with you. Ask them to talk about their play both during and after their play experiences.
- **Help children understand the difference between guessing and knowing.** A guess, or hypothesis, needs to be tested. Assist children with simple experiments in which they make predictions based on their hypotheses, gather evidence by making observations that they document (e.g., through pictures, dictated stories, graphs), and seek information to help them support or reject their original hypotheses and make conclusions. Do they prove their hypotheses, or do they need to do additional experimenting?
- **Foster categorization skills.** Provide materials that allow children to explore, compare, and sort by a variety of attributes (size, shape, sound, taste, etc.). With younger children, use objects that differ in just one attribute (e.g., balls of different colors). Ask children to describe the similarities and differences and to put the objects into categories. Use and reinforce vocabulary that helps children describe their comparisons (e.g.,

short, round, loud, quiet, blue, red, smooth, bumpy) and use problem-solving language (e.g., hypothesis, compare, observe, interpret). During play, notice how children use materials. Do they sort them? Do they comment on similarities and differences?
- **Encourage children to think before responding.** Help children learn to freeze—to take a moment before answering a question to think about their best or most reasonable response to a problem and how they would test it. With a group of children, discuss different ways they solved a problem to demonstrate that there is often more than one way to do so. Point out that children sometimes think about and approach things differently, but that everyone's ideas should be respected.
- **Model and promote scientific reasoning, using the language of problem solving.** Teachers demonstrate good habits of problem solvers when they encourage children to use their senses to observe the world around them, help children form questions about what they observe and make predictions, share their own thinking and problem-solving processes aloud with children, model and conduct experiments to test predictions, and facilitate discussion about the results of children's experiments.

making" by developing children's planning and reflecting skills (Epstein 2014). (See "Checklist of Teaching Practices and Strategies to Support Preschool Children's Problem Solving and Reasoning," for further explanation of strategies.)

Foster categorization skills. Understanding how to compare and contrast, categorize, and sort enables children to generalize information from one category or situation to another—to reason inductively (Hollister Sandberg & McCullough 2010). Generalizing helps children determine how to approach new objects or events with confidence. For example, 4-year-old Justin was once bitten by a dog and now is afraid of all dogs. During neighborhood walks, his parents have helped him categorize dogs by watching for behavioral signs: a dog with a wagging tail and relaxed demeanor is most likely friendly, but a dog that is barking and has its ears pinned back and teeth bared should be given some space. When they visit the park, Justin generalizes the information he learned about which dogs he can feel safe with based on how he categorizes their behavior.

To promote categorizing, provide children with objects or sets of objects that have contrasting qualities and encourage them to explain how the objects are alike and not alike (Loewenstein & Gentner 2001; Mix 2008; Christie & Gentner 2010). Challenge children to categorize by attributes beyond size and shape; for example, ask them to group objects according to color, width, or function (e.g., "find tools that can cut") (Kemler Nelson, Holt, & Egan 2004). Also, notice how children spontaneously categorize during play; what attributes are they using to categorize in sets they create?

Teachers also foster categorization skills by modeling strategies for children. Children as young as 3 can understand and imitate categorization strategies they see a teacher use without the teacher explicitly stating the strategies (Williamson & Markman 2006; Williamson, Meltzoff, & Markman 2008; Williamson, Jaswal, & Meltzoff 2010). For example, with a group of children watching, Sandy arranges several toys in front of her. Some of the toys make noise and some do not. Without telling children what characteristic she is using to sort, she carefully picks up each toy, shakes it and listens to it, and then puts the toy in the appropriate group. For the last few unsorted toys, she picks them up one at a time and says to a child, "Sort the toys the way I did." To do so, the child must have attended to what Sandy did, understood her goal, and learned her sorting rule as she modeled the strategy (shaking the toys and listening). This requires deeper-level mental processes and more complex problem solving than if Sandy had simply told the children her sorting rule.

Encourage children to brainstorm multiple solutions to problems. Young children tend to act on their first impulse in a situation or on the first thing that comes to mind. But to be good thinkers, they need to develop *inhibitory control*, "the ability to ignore distractions and stay focused, and to resist making one response and instead make another" (Diamond 2006). Inhibitory control helps children regulate their emotions and behavior and problem solve more effectively. Teachers can help children learn this important skill by encouraging them to pause before acting; consider multiple solutions to questions, tasks, or problems; and then choose a solution to try out.

Model and promote scientific reasoning. Scientific reasoning involves constructing hypotheses, gathering evidence, conducting experiments to test hypotheses, and drawing conclusions (Hollister Sandberg & McCullough 2010). It requires children to distinguish between various explanations for events and determine whether there is evidence to support the explanations. Although this is a complex type of reasoning for young children, teachers can support it through modeling and scaffolding. For example, after encouraging children to construct multiple reasonable explanations for events (hypotheses), teachers can help children talk through the steps they will take to test their hypotheses, as Sandy did in the first scenario with Keira and the slide. As children test their hypotheses, teachers should encourage them to use their senses (i.e., smell, touch, sight, sound, taste) to observe, gather, and record data (e.g., through pictures or charts). Finally, teachers can help children summarize the results of their investigation and construct explanations (i.e., verbalize cause and effect) for their findings. When teachers ask children questions such as "Why do you think that?" or "How do you know?," they help children become aware of their own thinking processes, reflect on the results of their experiments, and evaluate outcomes.

Conclusion

Children's ability to problem solve and reason is integral to their academic as well as social success. Each day, early childhood teachers support these skills in numerous ways—for example, by facilitating children's play, scaffolding learning, and offering interesting and challenging experiences. With a better understanding of how young children's reasoning and problem-solving skills develop, and a plan for implementing strategies to support them, teachers will become more intentional in helping children become good thinkers.

References

Amsterlaw, J., & H.M. Wellman. 2006. "Theories of Mind in Transition: A Microgenetic Study of the Development of False Belief Understanding." *Journal of Cognition and Development* 7 (2): 139–72.

Bierman, K.L., C.E. Domitrovich, R.L. Nix, S.D. Gest, J.A. Welsh, M.T. Greenberg, C. Blair, K.E. Nelson, & S. Gill. 2008. "Promoting Academic and Social-Emotional School Readiness: The Head Start REDI Program." *Child Development* 79 (6): 1802–17. www.ncbi.nlm.nih.gov/pubmed/19037591

Cannon, E.N., & A.L. Woodward. 2012. "Infants Generate Goal-Based Action Predictions." *Developmental Science* 15 (2): 292–98. www.ncbi.nlm.nih.gov/pubmed/22356184

Christie, S., & D. Gentner. 2010. "Where Hypotheses Come From: Learning New Relations by Structural Alignment." *Journal of Cognition and Development* 11(3): 356–73.

Denham, S.A., & C.M. Almeida. 1987. "Children's Social Problem-Solving Skills, Behavioral Adjustment, and Interventions: A Meta-Analysis Evaluating Theory and Practice." *Journal of Applied Developmental Psychology* 8 (4):391–409. http://nichcy.org/research/summaries/abstract29

Denham, S.A., H.H. Bassett, M. Mincic, S. Kalb, E. Way, T. Wyatt, & Y. Segal. 2012. "Social-Emotional Learning Profiles of Preschoolers' Early School Success: A Person-Centered Approach." *Learning and Individual Differences* 22 (2): 178–89. www.ncbi.nlm.nih.gov/pmc/ articles/PMC3294380

Diamond, A. 2006. "The Early Development of Executive Functions." Chap. 6 in *Lifespan Cognition: Mechanisms of Change,* eds. E. Bialystok & F.I.M. Craik, 70–95. New York: Oxford University Press.

Early, D., O. Barbarin, D. Bryant, M. Burchinal, F. Chang, R. Clifford, G.M. Crawford, C. Howes, S. Ritchie, M.E. Kraft-Sayre, R.C. Pianta, W.S. Barnett, & W. Weaver. 2005. "Pre-Kindergarten in Eleven States: NCEDL's Multi-State Study of Pre-Kindergarten & Study of State-Wide Early Education Programs (SWEEP): Preliminary Descriptive Report." NCEDL working paper. National Center for Early Development & Learning. http://fpg.unc.edu/sites/fpg.unc.edu/files/resources/reports-and-policy-briefs/NCEDL_PreK-in-Eleven-States_Working-Paper_2005.pdf

Epstein, A.S. 2014. *The Intentional Teacher: Choosing the Best Strategies for Young Children's Learning.* Rev. ed. Washington, DC: NAEYC.

Galinsky, E. 2010. *Mind in the Making: The Seven Essential Life Skills Every Child Needs.* New York: HarperCollins. Available from NAEYC.

Gopnik, A., C. Glymour, D.M. Sobel, L.E. Schulz, T. Kushnir, & D. Danks. 2004. "A Theory of Causal Learning in Children: Causal Maps and Bayes Nets." *Psychological Review* 111 (1):3–32. www.ncbi.nlm.nih.gov/pubmed/14756583

Critical Thinking

1. Prepare a list of strategies teachers can use in the classroom to foster problem solving skills.

2. Think how you would respond to a job interview question about what you might do in the classroom to encourage critical thinking and what are sometimes called executive functioning skills.

Internet References

Critical Thinking Foundation
http://www.criticalthinking.org/

Duke University: Talent Identification Program
http://tip.duke.edu/node/822

Early Childhood and Parenting Collaborative
http://ecap.crc.illinois.edu/eecearchive/digests/1993/britz93.html

JESSICA VICK WHITTAKER, PhD, is a research assistant professor at the Center for Advanced Teaching and Learning, University of Virginia, in Charlottesville. Her work focuses on developing and evaluating professional development aimed at improving teacher-child interaction quality to support children's math and science skills. She also studies children's self-regulation.

Article   Prepared by: Karen Menke Paciorek, *Eastern Michigan University*

10 Ways Kindergarten Can Stop Failing Our Kids

LAURIE LEVY

Learning Outcomes

After reading this article, you will be able to:

- Advocate for a child-centered environment in kindergarten.

- Explain to others the importance of kindergarten teachers being knowledgeable about child development.

- Discuss why social/emotional needs of five-year-olds are so important.

My grandson, like millions of other five- and six-year-olds across the country, is about to start his formal education in kindergarten. Like most kids, he's a bit worried. He has three important questions about what his new school will be like:

- Will my teacher be nice?
- Can I get cookies?
- Do they have a tiger robot in their toys?

Those are great, age-appropriate questions for a five-year-old to be asking, and I hope starting school brings him and his cohorts enough happy moments to fill those cute, overlarge backpacks they proudly carry around. But I'd be lying if I said I'm not a little worried for him, and for his peers—worried about our current educational climate and the demands it makes on these littlest learners.

Kindergarten has changed so much over the past decade; it is so much more work and so much less play. No Child Left Behind and Race to the Top have brought learning standards with higher (and not necessarily developmentally appropriate) expectations of these young children, and the partner of these standards, assessment, plays a huge role in today's kindergarten

classrooms. The validity of using this testing, often administered to five-year-olds before or at the very beginning of kindergarten, to track learning is questionable at best. Children this age aren't necessarily "test-ready": they may hesitate to answer a strange adult's questions, or prefer to stare out the window, and many don't understand that giving a complete answer actually matters. Sadly, it does.

In short, kindergarten has become the new first (or even second) grade, with kids anxiously filling in bubbles and receiving reading instruction when many can't even decode words yet. A dozen years ago, the play kitchens and imaginative free play areas disappeared, followed by the loss of blocks and easel paints and most other toys. Time for socialization and play has vanished. We seem to have forgotten that *how* children learn at this age matters—facts drilled into their heads that have no connection to their life experience, or regard for their development, are both meaningless and quickly forgotten. But it doesn't have to be that way.

Once upon a time we had a different vision for what the kindergarten year should be: a time for play and experimentation and the sorting out of self that leads to further learning. How can we create those kinds of learning environments again? Here are 10 ways schools can stop failing our kids in their earliest years, and begin building passionate learners from the start.

1. **Ensure time to learn through play and time to play for fun.** This should be obvious to educators who know anything about child development, but standards for what kids should know generally don't come with directions about the best way to teach them. Kids learn by doing, manipulating and playing. And in order to learn, they need time to play to recharge their batteries and discover important social skills.

2. **Grant permission to color outside of the lines.** Five-year-olds are amazingly creative if we allow them to express themselves. Worksheets and expectations of conformity undermine this. One of my granddaughters was berated in kindergarten for not finishing her "work" because she spent too much time coloring the pictures in the early squares. As my daughter explained it, she had no idea going fast was important—it never had been before.

3. **Employ educators who have patience with developing skills.** Zipping, shoe-tying, nose-wiping, opening lunch-foods, and even toileting independently can challenge a five-year-old. Many teachers have told me that dealing with these issues is the worst part about teaching kindergarten. So I wish the kindergarten class of 2015 teachers who both expect and don't mind these challenges.

4. **Understand that not all kindergarteners are going to be developmentally ready to read, write or take tests.** Even though we wish all kids could be readers and writers when they leave kindergarten, some will not be able to do this yet. And that's okay. When a child's mind is ready for reading, the light bulb goes on. Before then, the child is more of a parrot than a reader. Unless there is an underlying problem, kids learn to read when they are ready. There's no shame in not getting it until age 6, or even 7.

5. **Expect occasional squirrelly behavior.** It's really hard for these little kids to sit still all day doing work—and not all of them have ADHD and need to be medicated. Early childhood educators understand that kids need hours of free playtime from their earliest days to develop healthy sensory systems that enable their brains to learn. Valerie Strauss recently posted a piece on this issue by Angela Hanscom titled, *Why So Many Kids Can't Sit Still in School Today*. It's worth reading Hanscom's answer, as she is a pediatric occupational therapist as well as an advocate for more creative play in children's lives.

6. **Insist that teachers are trained in child development.** I always think of kindergarten as the year of sorting everything out. Children generally span over a year age-wise, from the child who just turned five to the child who is already six and was held back. Add to that the huge range of skills and social/emotional ability among children this age; the fact that there will be kids with special needs and learning challenges yet to be indentified; and the reality that, for some children, this is their first exposure to any kind of formal group learning, and you've got a challenging mix for any teacher to handle. The best tool a kindergarten teacher can possess is the ability to look at this wide range of behavior, development, experience, skill, and maturity through the eyes of someone well-trained in child development.

7. **Realize that the hardest parts of kindergarten have little to do with academic learning (parents too!).** Arrival, lunch, recess, transitions, bathroom routines, and rules in general are really challenging for children this age. Untrained personnel who often have little patience for the needs of five- and six-year-olds often supervise arrival and lunch times. Recess (if allowed) can resemble *Lord of the Flies,* as kids with developing social skills are left pretty much on their own to negotiate peer interactions. The rules in general often don't make sense to kindergarteners. In particular, many have trouble figuring out when it is okay to use the bathroom, leading to accidents. If there are specialists (gym, music, art, drama, etc.), these teachers will have different rules and not really know the kids as well as their kindergarten teacher. All in all, it's a lot to manage for such young children.

8. **Develop a kindergarten curriculum that meets the developmental and social/emotional needs of 5-year-old learners.** Kindergarten is definitely the year to differentiate expectations and instruction, as there will be huge differences in what children know and how they behave. The curriculum should still be based in early childhood best practices, not merely a push down of what was formerly first or second grade work. Teaching kids in large groups and expecting them to sit for long periods of time is unrealistic. Learning activity stations and play-based activities are definitely the way to go.

9. **Welcome parents as part of a team working in the best interests of the child.** Parents must advocate for their young children because they cannot do it themselves. School principals need to be available to parents and require teachers to listen when parents share anything unique about their child's needs, learning style, behavior, or life situation. Asking for and allowing help from parents will benefit everyone.

10. **Be sensitive to the child who is chronologically young or has special needs.** Among my eight grandkids, I have both issues. Two of the boys have June birthdays, which can be a disadvantage these days because of kids who are red-shirted (held back) and current educational expectations that may not be developmentally appropriate, especially for the youngest students. And kids with special needs who are included in general education classes still have different learning and social challenges that must be understood and addressed. School

districts need to avoid pressuring teachers to expect all children to meet standards at the same pace and time, thus ensuring better test scores. And teachers need to walk the talk of differentiated instruction, and be especially empathic to those who may struggle due to age or ability.

Getting back to my grandson's three questions about kindergarten: with regret, I've informed him that cookies will not be served for snack (unhealthy), and there will not be tiger robots in the classroom (in fact, there probably won't be any toys). But I hope I will eventually be able to respond with a resounding yes to his first question: Will the teacher be nice? In fact, I expect the teacher to honor my grandson's energy, curiosity, zest for life, and unique interests. I'm not really worried about how much "stuff" he learns. I simply want him to learn to love learning, and be happy, as he begins his formal education. That's what kindergarten should be all about.

Critical Thinking

1. What would you add to the list Levy developed?
2. How would you help parents of a soon-to-be kindergartener prepare their child for kindergarten? What do children need to be able to do to be successful in kindergarten?

Internet References

Association for Childhood Education International
http://acei.org/

National Association for the Education of Young Children
http://naeyc.org/

PBS Parents
http://www.pbs.org/parents/education/going-to-school/grade-by-grade/kindergarten/

Article   Prepared by: Karen Menke Paciorek, *Eastern Michigan University*

Supporting Children's Learning While Meeting State Standards

Strategies and Suggestions for Pre-K–Grade 3 Teachers in Public School Contexts.

In Jenny Aster's kindergarten classroom, the 30-minute "literacy stations" block is coming to a close. Stragglers finish their daily journal entries, put their completed handwriting worksheets in the All Done basket, and staple the *at* word family booklets they've created. Jenny claps rhythmically to get the children's attention: "It's time to clean up so we can have centers. The quicker we clean up, the sooner we can start." The children scurry around the room picking up scraps of paper and returning supplies to their proper locations.

When center time begins, it is easy to see why the children were so motivated to get started. The centers transform the space from a teacher-directed environment to a buffet of child-directed learning opportunities. A pair of bland, unmarked cupboard doors swings open to reveal a large assortment of unit blocks, all of which are eagerly—and noisily—pulled onto the speckled linoleum floor and immediately used to construct a racing tower. Several robber–pirates dart out of the housekeeping area, scarves tied around their heads and clutching treasure-filled sacks. Children pull puzzles and games onto the carpet, reminding each other of the rules and procedures.

A businesslike group of clipboard-holding girls moves purposefully through the room, engaging briefly with each small group of busy children. The girls apologize for interrupting, ask a few questions, make notes, and move on. A quick peek at their clipboards reveals each girl using invented spelling and cues from environmental print, such as entries on the classroom word wall, to record classmates' names and responses.

Lisa S. Goldstein and Michelle Bauml

Learning Outcomes

After reading this article, you will be able to:

- Identify three traits common to teachers who successfully balance an understanding of the students' needs with curricular demands.

- Describe three strategies presented in the article that would enhance teaching and learning.

The current emphasis on standards-based education and accountability in public schools in the United States has had a significant impact on early childhood teachers' practices. States, school districts, and administrators may require teachers to cover certain academic content standards and/or use particular instructional materials. But many teachers at the prekindergarten, kindergarten, and primary grade levels are concerned about the ways in which these new expectations limit their ability to meet the needs of individual children and to promote the learning of all the children they teach (Goldstein 2007a, 2007b; Valli & Buese 2007).

Asking teachers to stop making decisions about what to teach and how best to teach it is as unrealistic as asking artists to stop choosing which colors to use on their canvas: making intentional decisions about curriculum and instruction is the signature responsibility that defines teaching as a profession (Hawthorne 1992). Even when school districts enact policies with explicit expectations for curriculum content and instructional practices, teachers rarely follow those lesson plans or pacing guides exactly as they are written (Ehly 2009); early childhood educators seek every available opportunity to provide meaningful, engaging learning experiences that support all children (DeVault 2003; Geist & Baum 2005; Bauml 2008).

Early childhood educators seek every available opportunity to provide meaningful, engaging learning experiences that support all children.

Most public school teachers have a repertoire of strategies for modifying the requirements in ways that allow them to do what they know will be most effective in advancing children's learning. Perhaps they replace the storybook suggested in the Teachers' Edition with one they believe to be more suitable. Or they incorporate sheltered instructional strategies, such as the use of visual aids or concrete materials to support dual language learners' comprehension of the academic content in a science lesson. They might supplement a required mathematics lesson on addition with a range of math games that help children practice and integrate the concepts introduced in the lesson. Maybe their administrators have given them permission to make these departures from their districts' policies and expectations. Possibly they have colleagues with whom they discuss and share strategies for tweaking the required plans.

Our goal in this article is to bring these strategies into the open. We encourage all pre-K–grade 3 teachers to consider their need to develop effective strategies for teaching state standards in appropriate, responsive ways as a challenge to be embraced explicitly and overtly. In discussions about the findings of our individual research projects—Lisa's with experienced kindergarten teachers (Goldstein 2007a, 2007b, 2008) and Michelle's with preservice teachers in grades pre-K–grade 4 (Bauml 2008, 2009)—we identified three traits common to those teachers who successfully balance "the child and the curriculum" (Dewey 1902) in today's complex public school environments. These teachers acquire detailed and thorough knowledge of the policies, procedures, and requirements shaping their work; they consider the district-adopted materials to be a starting point for curriculum and instruction; and they actively showcase children's learning and academic progress. In this article we discuss each of these traits, providing examples and suggestions to help all early childhood teachers find new ways to work within existing constraints and to continue to make the decisions about curriculum and instruction that will be most beneficial to young learners.

Trait 1: Acquire Detailed and Thorough Knowledge of Policies and Expectations

A strong knowledge base is essential for making effective decisions. Today it may seem that new obligations, demands, and expectations are coming at teachers from all directions. Having the information you need, being clear about requirements, and understanding the implications of the policies shaping your practice allow you to make curricular and instructional decisions that meet the needs of the children you teach, as well as the expectations of your school or district. Here are a few ways to develop your knowledge base:

Know the Law

Build a strong understanding of the relevant aspects of the federal and state legislation governing your practices. Your curricular and instructional decisions should be principled and intentional (Epstein 2007), grounded in the real details of the laws that govern your responsibilities. You can find information about state policy on your state education agency website, and information about federal requirements at the US Department of Education's website (www.ed.gov) or in books written to inform parents, teachers, and others about the details and demands of recent education policies and reform efforts (David & Cuban 2010).

The long list of content standards in each area of the curriculum can seem daunting, but there are ways to manage the scope of this endeavor.

Know Your State's Content Standards

In classrooms from pre-K to grade 12, public school teachers are expected to move their students to mastery of their state's content standards. A detailed, thorough knowledge of exactly which skills and what knowledge comprise the content standards makes this goal much more attainable. The long list of content standards in each area of the curriculum can seem daunting, but there are ways to manage the scope of this endeavor. For example, grade level study groups can explore the state standards for each content area in greater depth (Ehly 2009). During this exploration, study group members might make note of cross-disciplinary connections that can create and enhance standards-based thematic curriculum units (Helm 2008).

Article   Prepared by: Karen Menke Paciorek, *Eastern Michigan University*

Time to Play:
Recognizing the Benefits of Recess

CATHERINE RAMSTETTER AND ROBERT MURRAY

Learning Outcomes

After reading this article, you will be able to:

- Identify the role of play in children's development.

- Advocate for recess for all children every day.

- Explain how daily recess can improve academic performance.

One sunny day in May, Ms. Brown tells her first-grade class, "OK, boys and girls, it's time for recess." As the children leave the classroom in an organized fashion, three other first-grade classes join them out on the playground, an open field with one tree and a six-foot-tall monkey bar structure. Under the teachers' watchful eye, the children climb and play.

After 15 min, one of the teachers blows a whistle, and the children run back to the building, where another teacher leads them in. Aside from a few latecomers to the door, every child has entered the building in less than 30 s. Back in the classroom, Ms. Brown begins a song about not dawdling, and the children move to the carpet for a group story discussion.

Earlier that day, Ms. Brown wasn't so sure all of her students should go to recess. Connor had acted out one too many times, and she was thinking he didn't deserve to go out and play. But then, she remembered her training last spring and summer with LiiNK trainers (a project described later in this article), who urged her not to withhold recess as punishment.

So when recess arrived, Ms. Brown decided to allow Connor to go out; she even let him be the first student out the door. The break from his desk ends up helping him refocus. Upon returning to the classroom, Connor apologizes to Ms. Brown and promises to behave better. She believes it. The rest of the day is pleasant for her and Connor—indeed, for the whole class.

While denying recess to a misbehaving student is common for many teachers, Ms. Brown's response may not be. Her decision to allow Connor to attend recess and his subsequent apology show the power of unstructured play time for students during school.

What Is Recess?

The American Academy of Pediatrics (AAP), in its 2013 policy statement titled "The Crucial Role of Recess in School," describes recess as "a necessary break in the day for optimizing a child's social, emotional, physical, and cognitive development."[1] Recess ought to be safe and well supervised, yet teachers do not have to direct student activity. The frequency and duration of breaks should allow time for children to mentally decompress, and schools should allow students to experience recess periods daily.

As the AAP makes clear, outdoor play "can serve as a counterbalance to sedentary time and contribute to the recommended 60 min of moderate to vigorous activity per day."[2] An effective recess is one where children demonstrate their ability to stay within the boundaries of their play space, negotiate conflict with each other, and then return to academic learning. The peer interactions that take place during recess allow for communication, cooperation, and problem solving, complementing the classroom experience.[3] Unstructured play, with adult supervision, gives children the opportunity to develop important social and emotional skills, which is essential to a well-rounded education.

The AAP's policy statement on the role of recess in school cited four critical benefits of recess: (1) greater levels of physical activity and fitness, (2) improved attentiveness in class, (3) improved cognition and learning, and (4) practice of peer-to-peer social and emotional skills. The latter, often overlooked, is cited by child development experts as a fundamental skill set, laying the basis for social success in later life. As a result, the AAP concluded that "recess should be considered a child's personal time, and it should not be withheld for academic or punitive reasons."[4]

After all, "it is the supreme seriousness of play that gives it its educational importance," said Joseph Lee, the father of the playground movement. "Play seen from the inside, as the child sees it, is the most serious thing in life . . . Play builds the child . . . Play is thus the essential part of education."[5]

A Harvard-educated author and philanthropist, Lee advocated for playgrounds in city schools and parks in the late 19th and early 20th century. He was a leader in promoting school attendance and safe havens for play for all children, especially poor children in the urban core of Boston. In the 1890s, children were forbidden from playing games in the streets and there were no playgrounds in the poorest neighborhoods, where adolescent boys were routinely arrested for delinquency. Lee was from a wealthy Boston family, and, recalling the childhood he experienced—one filled with games, dancing, and play—he took it upon himself to find a solution. He gained permission to clear a vacant lot and provide materials and equipment he felt children would be likely to play with or on, such as dirt piles, large pipes, and sand. And, as he predicted, children came to play.

Over the next decades, Lee's initiative spread from Boston to Chicago and extended into municipal investment in parks and recreation centers for boys and girls. Lee's efforts also extended to public education. He was determined that poor children receive the same kind of educational opportunity in schools as their more affluent peers by being educated by teachers who were trained as teachers. He personally underwrote the creation of Harvard University's School of Education in 1920. It was during this period of growth in urban education and play space for children that recess—as a time during the school day for children to play in a designated space—came to be.[6]

Lee's vision of play in education still resonates today. Given that the new federal Every Student Succeeds Act (ESSA) removes the emphasis on high-stakes standardized testing in schools and includes nonacademic indicators as a component of a student's "well-rounded education,"[7] schools that have narrowly focused on scores to the detriment of students' well-being can now correct the imbalance. In doing so, they can ensure that recess, which plays a vital role in social and emotional development, maintains its rightful place in the school day.

The Current State of Recess

Beyond Lee's advocacy of playgrounds and recreation, it is difficult to document a precise history of recess. In fact, when the School Health Policies and Programs Study (SHPPS) was initiated in 1994 by the Centers for Disease Control and Prevention (CDC) with the purpose of providing "the first in-depth description of policies and programs related to multiple components of the school health program at the state, district, school, and classroom levels,"[8] recess was not included.

It wasn't until 1997 that the CDC defined recess as "regularly scheduled periods within the elementary school day for unstructured physical activity and play."[9] Recess was first included in the 2000 SHPPS, among various opportunities in schools for children to engage in physical activity. Prior to that, what we know about recess as an experience during the school day—an experience of childhood—is something that is informed by individual and collective memories.

Since then, in addition to SHPPS, other published research about recess practices and policies in the United States has included studies on a smaller scale, in a school or district. These explore various aspects of recess, under the assumption that recess is given for every child in that school or district.[10] Few studies, however, actually examine how recess varies within and across schools and districts (for instance, how teachers monitor and handle recess in the same school and grade).

Largely, the documentation of what happens in the daily, lived experience of recess in schools remains uneven and takes the form of blog posts, news stories, and other social media sharing. The limitations of understanding the delivery and experience of recess at individual schools aside, since the mid- to late-1990s, a growing body of evidence has emerged about the value of and practices and policies related to physical activity—of which recess is one part. Since its inception in 1994, SHPPS has been repeated in 2000, 2006, 2012, and 2014.

According to SHPPS data from 2014, "82.8 percent of elementary schools provided daily recess for students in all grades in the school."[11] (For a summary of current recess practices, see the table to the right.) Because this study surveys principals and "lead health education teachers," this statistic doesn't necessarily paint a complete picture of where, when, or how recess is provided,* and the documentation about current practices only includes data collected from those schools that reported having regularly scheduled recess. Even with these limitations, however, the 2014 SHPPS research is useful. It shows that, among elementary schools with regularly scheduled recess, the percentage of schools providing recess decreases from first to sixth grade. The average number of days with recess per week across all grades was 4.9, and the average time spent in recess was 26.9 minutes per day.

Decisions about timing, duration, location, and activities for recess are typically made at the school or grade level. While there is no recommended duration (minutes per day) or timing for

---

*To see the original questionnaires given to principals and teachers, visit www.cdc.gov/healthyyouth/data/profiles/questionnaires.htm.

Elementary School Recess by the Numbers

PRACTICE	ELEMENTARY SCHOOLS
Students participate in regularly scheduled recess during the school day in[1]	
Kindergarten	94.9%
First grade	95.0%
Second grade	94.7%
Third grade	94.3%
Fourth grade	93.3%
Fifth grade	90.6%
Sixth grade	34.9%
Average number of minutes students spend in recess each day[2]	26.9
Staff prohibited or actively discouraged from excluding students from all or part of recess as punishment for bad behavior or failure to complete classwork	54.4%
Recess structure	
Students engage in free play or physical activity	93.1%
Students are required or encouraged to use physical activity or fitness stations	2.8%
Other	4.0%
Recess is held outdoors, weather permitting	100%
When recess cannot be held outside	
Students participate in physical activity in the gymnasium, a multipurpose room, or the cafeteria	29.8%
Students participate in physical activity in regular classrooms	17.9%
Students watch a DVD/video[3]	5.8%
Students engage in other sedentary activities (e.g., board games)	39.5%
Other	7.0%

[1]Among elementary schools with students in that grade.
[2]Among schools in which students participate in regularly scheduled recess.
[3]Does not include physical activity DVDs/videos.

Source: School Health Policies And Practices Study, *Results From The School Health Policies and Practices Study* 2014 (Atlanta: Centers for Disease Control and Prevention, 2015), 50.

recess, one of the largest studies published on recess found that for 8- to 9-year-olds, at least one or more daily recess periods of at least 15 min was associated with better class behavior ratings from teachers than no daily recess or fewer minutes of recess.[12]

According to SHPPS data from 2000 to 2014, among schools that offer recess, the percentage of classes having regularly scheduled recess immediately after lunch decreased from 42.3 percent in 2000 to 26.2 percent in 2014. This may be a result of a decrease in recess opportunities, or it may reflect schools shifting recess times to before lunch, which has been shown to increase meal consumption and decrease food waste, while improving lunchroom behavior and increasing attention in the classroom following lunch.[13]

A comparison of results from the SHPPS surveys in 2006 and 2014 also indicates an alarming trend: in 2006, 96.8 percent of elementary schools provided recess for at least one grade in the school, compared with 82.8 percent in 2014. Using self-reported data from high-level administrators at the district level, these surveys show that even though more than 80 percent of districts claim to provide daily recess, a 2014 analysis conducted by the CDC and the Bridging the Gap research program revealed that 60 percent of districts had no policy regarding daily recess for elementary school students and that only 20 percent mandated daily recess.

Additionally, a 2006 analysis by the National Center for Education Statistics found noticeable disparities[14]:

- City schools reported the lowest average minutes per day of recess (24 min in first grade to 21 min in sixth grade).
- Rural schools reported the highest average minutes per day (31 min in first grade to 24 min in sixth grade).
- The lowest minutes per day of recess (21 min in first grade to 17 min in sixth grade) occurred in schools where 75 percent or more of the students were eligible for free or reduced-price lunch.

Decreased opportunities for recess have been associated with increased academic pressure. Recess has been the victim of the perceived need to spend more time preparing students for standardized testing and, generally, to meet increased demands for instructional time. Diminishing recess first began in the early 1990s, and it further declined with the enactment of No Child Left Behind in 2001, which emphasized English language arts and mathematics. To focus on these core areas, districts reduced time for recess, art, music, physical education, and even lunch.[15] In addition, recess often was and is withheld from students as punishment for disruptive behavior and/or to encourage task completion, even though research shows this practice "deprives students of health benefits important to their well-being."[16]

Interestingly, the emergence of a national health crisis in the United States—the rising rates of obesity in children—has sparked a reevaluation of recess. Recess was included, along with physical education and other opportunities for school-based physical activity, in the wellness policy requirement enacted in 2004 as part of the Child Nutrition and Special Supplemental Nutrition Program for Women, Infants, and Children Reauthorization Act.* (But, as we just noted, a recess-specific policy is lacking in 40 percent of school districts.) In 2014, this requirement was bolstered by an approved rule under the Healthy, Hunger-Free Kids Act of 2010,[17] which "expands the requirements to strengthen policies and increase transparency. The responsibility for developing, implementing, and evaluating a wellness policy is placed at the local level, so the unique needs of each school under the [district's] jurisdiction can be addressed."[18] By June 30, 2017, all schools/districts must have a wellness policy that meets all required components.

In conjunction with these federal initiatives, some state legislatures have explored recess as part of a broader school-based wellness or physical activity education bill. Accurately documenting what these legislative actions mean for recess is difficult, partially because recess could fall under a variety of

laws or policies, and also because the way the law or policy is written can vary. (For example, a mandate may require a set number of minutes per day for physical activity, with recess included, or it might require recess be specifically included in a district wellness policy.)

To supplement CDC and SHPPS information, the National Association of State Boards of Education's State School Health Policy Database is updated as states enact or revise laws and policies. Within states, districts can add to or build on any federal or state requirement.† A similar database does not exist for district-level school health policies, but as indicated by Bridging the Gap's research, such policies often do not include recess.

With the renewed emphasis on a "well-rounded education," thanks to ESSA, states and schools now have additional incentive to elevate policies and practices for regular recess as part of a robust package of "nonacademic" health and physical activity initiatives, which research has shown to positively affect academic progress.

ESSA requires states to select at least one nonacademic indicator that each school district will report. Funds for implementing the federal law will be allocated to the states to distribute, and they include funds for professional development and programs to support students' physical health as well as their mental and behavioral health. Recess offers a unique way to address both.

Integrating Recess into School Culture

In 2011, the Chicago Public Schools (CPS) announced it would reintroduce daily recess in the 2012 school year, making it "the first large urban district to once again require daily recess at the elementary and middle school levels."[19] This move was prompted by a groundswell of parents, community members, and concerned district employees, who led the push for recess reinstatement during their struggle to lengthen the school day. We could find no published accounts on the decision to eliminate recess in the first place; however, based on the timing (recess was discontinued in the early 1980s), we can surmise it was both a cost-cutting measure and a response to concerns that students spend as much time as possible on academics.

Thus, in the fall of 2012, when CPS extended the school day by at least 30 min across the district, recess once again became a daily occurrence at all elementary and middle schools. Exactly

---

*The wellness policy language only includes recess as one of the ways schools can address student physical activity. Schools are only required to have a policy that addresses nutrition services, nutrition education, physical education, and physical activity. The federal law does not prescribe the duration, timing, or type of activities. Some states have laws, some have recommendations that are codified, and some have nothing (which is the case for recess in most states).
†For a state-by-state listing of recess policies in schools, see www.nasbe.org/healthy_schools/hs/bytopics.php?topicid=3120.

how these minutes are used varies at each school, but reinstating recess did not take away instructional time. Once recess was reinstated, the CPS Office of Student Health and Wellness codified daily recess by making it a provision of the district's Local School Wellness Policy that was passed in 2012, which mandates that all CPS K-8 students receive a minimum of 20 min of recess each day.[20] The office provides ongoing support for teachers and administrative personnel to engage in daily recess and other wellness practices. Reinstating recess not only required dedicating the time for it but also required training and resources for schools and teachers to ensure it was safe and consistent across a large number of schools in a wide variety of neighborhoods.

More recently, in September 2015, the Seattle Public Schools and the local teachers union agreed to a guaranteed minimum of 30 min of daily recess for elementary school students, although teachers had originally asked for 45 min.[21]

Such changes in recess require schools to rearrange schedules. But even in districts where recess is required, how students experience it is sharply inequitable, as demonstrated at Detroit's Spain Elementary-Middle School, where "students are forced to walk the halls during recess, because the gym is shut down due to mold and the outdoor playground emits burning steam—even during Detroit snowstorms."[22]‡ Children in poverty also have less access to free play, fewer minutes of physical activity during the day, and the fewest minutes of recess in school.[23]

Promising Programs

Ongoing research continues to expand our understanding of why recess and play are crucial. Some studies are exploring play spaces, specific activities, and the benefits of close supervision, while others are examining the benefits of accumulated physical activity and social interactions. While much is being learned from practices in other countries, three programs in the United States are particularly instructive: Peaceful Playgrounds, Playworks, and the Let''s Inspire Innovation 'N Kids (LiiNK) Project out of Texas Christian University.* Each offers a slightly different philosophy and approach, but the commonalities are that recess is well supervised and that every child experiences daily, safe play time during the school day. Each program is annually evaluated, and findings have demonstrated the benefits of recess as a component of a whole-child education.

Peaceful Playgrounds began in 1995 and is grounded in the following principles: teaching conflict resolution, establishing clear rules and expectations, providing low-cost equipment,

and designing a play space that invites exploration and interaction and minimizes potential for conflict. Peaceful Playgrounds offers training for school personnel in the wealth of games available to children and provides blueprints, playground stencils, and playground game guides. The program emphasizes free choice by students.

Playworks, which began in 1996 as Sports4Kids, focuses on using safe play and physical activity during recess and throughout the day to improve the climate at low-income schools. The program offers a variety of services that hinge on training or providing Playworks "coaches" to "enhance and transform recess and play into a positive experience that helps students and teachers get the most out of every learning opportunity." According to a survey of Playworks schools, staff report a decrease in bullying and disciplinary incidents, an increase in students' physical activity during recess, and an increase in students' abilities to focus on class activities.[24]

The *LiiNK Project*, a school curriculum modeled after one in Finland (whose academic performance consistently ranks in the top five countries in the world—well above the United States), was created three years ago to balance a focus on academics and the social and emotional health of children and teachers. Ms. Brown, the first-grade teacher mentioned earlier, teaches in a LiiNK school.

While LiiNK received national media attention in 2016 as strictly a recess program, it emphasizes more than just embedding additional recess into the school day. It also focuses on preparing teachers and administrators to redesign learning environments through recess, character education, and teacher training, in order to combat critical issues affecting the development of noncognitive skills, such as empathy in students.[25] Preliminary pilot data are compelling: in schools implementing the LiiNK curriculum, student achievement significantly improved, as did students' listening, decision-making, and problem-solving abilities.[26]

Other recess practices, both in the United States and in other countries, have demonstrated positive effects for students and teachers. As discussed previously, the move to conduct recess before lunch is associated with decreased food waste, increased consumption of fruits and vegetables, and better behavior in the lunchroom and upon returning to the classroom.

In studies with British children, providing large equipment and playground markings increased physical activity levels.[27] A study in Belgium found a similar effect on physical activity levels through providing smaller, less costly games and equipment.[28] Across the globe, simply providing these kinds of

---

‡For more on health and safety in schools, see "A Matter of Health and Safety" in the Winter 2016–2017 issue of American Educator, available at www.aft.org/ae/winter2016-2017/roseman.

*For more about the programs described here. See www.peacefulplaygrounds.com, www.playworks.org, and www.linkproject.tcu.edu.

portable play Equipment, such as balls and jump ropes, encourages children to be active during recess.[29]

Holding recess outside invites self-directed play where children choose what to do, from playing make-believe games, to reading or daydreaming, to socializing and engaging in physically active games; the experience is up to the child. Certainly, these activities can also occur in an indoor setting, but the opportunity for exploration is limited.[30] Interestingly, a large controlled study in China found that outdoor recess may help prevent or minimize nearsightedness in children.[31]

Meanwhile, children in Japan experience recess in 5- to 10-min bouts approximately every hour, based on the premise that a child's attention span wanes after 40–50 minutes of academic instruction.[32]

Given the evidence of the value of recess for children and teachers, what can educators, schools, and districts do to promote this critical aspect of the education of the whole child? Daily decisions about who gets recess and when and where it will happen are often made by teachers; thus, teachers are a crucial link for recess. Policies that support daily recess for all children are also essential, especially when it comes to the practice of withholding some or all of recess for disciplinary reasons.[33]

It is imperative to treat recess time as a child's personal time (similar to the way adults take breaks and choose how to spend them) and to make this explicit in policy and in practice. Recess time should not be usurped to fulfill a physical activity requirement. That is, if the school is required to offer opportunities outside of physical education classes, recess should only be included as an optional or supplemental opportunity. During recess, it should be as acceptable for children to engage in other types of play as it is for them to engage in physical activity. In addition to policy, teachers, administrators, and school staff would benefit from coursework during initial preparation, as well as from ongoing professional development, in recess management and in establishing and carrying out alternatives to discipline other than withholding recess.

Other ways to promote recess include:

- Advocating for district and school policies that require or recommend daily recess for every child.
- Disseminating information on the benefits of recess and the successful programs and practices described above.
- Including recess-type games and the practice of conflict resolution in physical education teacher training and in school physical education curricula.[†]

- Encouraging state and district boards of education to integrate the social and emotional benefits of recess in health education curricula.
- Collaborating with school wellness councils, school health and wellness teams, and parent–teacher groups to reinforce policies for recess, fund the purchase and maintenance of playground or recess equipment, and train playground monitors and teachers.

Daily recess for every child supports a school's mission of providing a high-quality, comprehensive, and meaningful education, so student grow and reach their full potential. Participating in recess offers children the necessary break to optimize their social, emotional, physical, and cognitive development. It not only helps them get important daily physical activity but also requires them to engage in rule-making, rule-following, and conflict resolution with peers. These are essential life skills that children can learn to master through the serious act of play.

Notes

1. American Academy of Pediatrics, "Policy Statement: The Crucial Role of Recess in School," Pediatrics 131, no. 1 (2013): 186.
2. American Academy of Pediatrics, "Policy Statement," 186.
3. American Academy of Pediatrics, "Policy Statement," 186.
4. American Academy of Pediatrics, "Policy Statement," 186.
5. Joseph Lee, *Play in Education* (New York: Macmillan, 1915), 3–7.
6. The history of Joseph Lee's life is informed by Donald Culross Peattie, *Lives of Destiny: As Told for the "Reader's Digest"* (Boston: Houghton Mifflin, 1954), 80–88.
7. Every Student Succeeds Act, Pub. L. No. 114–95, § 8002(21), 129 Stat 2099 (2015).
8. Lloyd J. Kolbe, Laura Kann, Janet L. Collins, Meg Leavy Small, Beth Collins Pateman, and Charles W. Warren, "The School Health Policies and Programs Study (SHPPS): Context, Methods, General Findings, and Future Efforts," *Journal of School Health* 65 (1995): 339.
9. *Promoting Better Health for Young People through Physical Activity and Sports* (Washington, DC: U.S. Department of Health and Human Services and U.S. Department of Education), app. 7, accessed January 19, 2017, www.thenewpe.com/advocacy/promotingPA.pdf.
10. A notable exception explored the effects of recess in one classroom in a school that had eliminated recess. See Olga S. Jarrett, Darlene M. Maxwell, Carrie Dickerson, Pamela Hoge, Gwen Davies, and Amy Yetley, "Impact of Recess

[†]Physical education is intended to impart not only sport-specific physical and competition skills but also lifelong physical health skills, like rule and goal setting, rule following, and general fine and gross motor skills. While separate from recess, physical education is one class that offers a place where children can learn recess-type games, or games that require imagination and physical movement, as well as appropriate ways to negotiate conflict with others.

on Classroom Behavior: Group Effects and Individual Differences," *Journal of Eccducational Research* 92 (1998): 121–126.

11. Centers for Disease Control and Prevention, "School Health Policies and Practices Study: 2014 Overview" (Atlanta: U.S. Department of Health and Human Services, 2015), 1.

12. Romina M. Barros, Ellen J. Silver, and Ruth E. K. Stein, "School Recess and Group Classroom Behavior," *Pediatrics* 123 (2009): 431–436.

13. Ethan A. Bergman, Nancy S. Buergel, Annaka Femrite, Timothy F. Englund, and Michael R. Braunstein, *Relationship of Meal and Recess Schedules to Plate Waste in Elementary Schools* (University, MS: National Food Service Management Institute, 2003); Montana Office of Public Instruction School Nutrition Programs, *Pilot Project Report: A Recess before Lunch Policy in Four Montana Schools, April 2002–May 2003* (Helena: Montana Office of Public Instruction, 2003); and Joseph Price and David Just, "Lunch, Recess and Nutrition: Responding to Time Incentives in the Cafeteria" (paper, Social Science Research Network, December 9, 2014), doi: 10.2139/ssrn.2536103.

14. Basmat Parsad and Laurie Lewis, *Calories In, Calories Out: Food and Exercise in Public Elementary Schools, 2005* (Washington, DC: National Center for Education Statistics, 2006), 62.

15. Jennifer McMurrer, *Instructional Time in Elementary Schools: A Closer Look at Changes for Specific Subjects*, From the Capital to the Classroom: Year 5 of the No Child Left Behind Act (Washington, DC: Center on Education Policy, 2008).

16. Centers for Disease Control and Prevention, "Guidelines for School and Community Programs to Promote Lifelong Physical Activity among Young People," *Morbidity and Mortality Weekly Report* 46, no. RR-6 (March 7, 1997): 12.

17. Healthy, Hunger-Free Kids Act of 2010, Pub. L. No. 111-296, § 204, 124 Stat. 3216 (2010).

18. "Local School Wellness Policy Implementation under the Healthy, Hunger-Free Kids Act of 2010: Summary of the Final Rule," U.S. Department of Agriculture, July 2016, accessed December 15, 2016, www.fns.usda.gov/sites/default/files/tn/LWPsummary_finalrule.pdf.

19. "CPS' Daily Recess Is More Than Just Play," Healthy Schools Campaign, February 17, 2015, www.healthyschools campaign.org/chicago-focus/cps-daily-recess-is-more-thanjust-play-5395.

20. "Local School Wellness Policy for Students," Chicago· Public Schools Policy Handbook, § 704.7, October 24, 2012, http://policy.cps.edu/download.aspx?ID=81.

21. Rachel Lerman, "Seattle District, Teachers Agree to Higher Pay for Subs, Longer Recess, but Strike Could Still Happen," *Seattle Times*, September 6, 2015.

22. Katie Felber, "Heartbreaking Video Depicts Harsh Reality of Detroit Public Schools," Good, January 19, 2016, www.good.is/videos/heartbreaking-video-detroit-public-schools.

23. Parsad and Lewis, *Calories In, Calories Out.*

24. "2016 Annual Survey Results—National," Playworks, accessed December 8, 2016, www.playworks.org/about/annual-survey/national.

25. Debbie Rhea, "Recess: The Forgotten Classroom," *Instructional Leader* 29, no. 1 (January 2016): 1.

26. Rhea, "Recess"; and Deborah J. Rhea, Alexander P. Rivchun, and Jacqueline Pennings, "The Liink Project: Implementation of a Recess and Character Development Pilot Study with Grades K & 1 Children," *Texas Association for Health, Physical Education, Recreation & Dance Journal* 84, no. 2 (Summer 2016): 14–17, 35.

27. Nicola D. Ridgers, Gareth Stratton, Stuart J. Fairclough, and Jos W. R. Twisk, "Long-Term Effects of a Playground Markings and Physical Structures on Children's Recess Physical Activity Levels," *Preventative Medicine* 44 (2007): 393–397.

28. Stefanie J. M. Verstraete, Greet M. Cardon, Dirk L. R. De Clercq, and Ilse M. M. De Bourdeaudhuij, "Increasing Children's Physical Activity Levels during Recess Periods in Elementary Schools: The Effects of Providing Game Equipment," *European Journal of Public Health* 16 (2006): 415–419.

29. Nicola D. Ridgers, Jo Salmon, Anne-Maree Parrish, Rebecca M. Stanley, and Anthony D. Okely, "Physical Activity during School Recess: A Systematic Review," *American Journal of Preventive Medicine* 43 (2012): 327.

30. Deborah J. Rhea and Irene Nigaglioni, "Outdoor Playing= Outdoor Learning," *Educational Facility Planner* 49, nos. 2–3 (2016): 16–20.

31. Mingguang He, Fan Xiang, Yangfa Zeng, et al., "Effect of Time Spent Outdoors at School on the Development of Myopia among Children in China: A Randomized Clinical Trial," *JAMA* 314, no. 11 (2015): 1142–1148.

32. Harold W. Stevenson and Shin-Ying Lee, "Contexts of Achievement: A Study of American, Chinese, and Japanese Children," *Monographs of the Society for Research in Child Development* 55, nos. 1–2 (1990).

33. Lindsey Turner, Jamie F. Chriqui, and Frank J. Chaloupka, "Withholding Recess from Elementary School Students: Policies Matter," *Journal of School Health* 83 (2013): 533–541.

Critical Thinking

1. Reflect on time you spent in recess as an elementary school child. What was the amount of time each day? What did you spend most of your time doing?

2. Talk to parents about the experiences their elementary school children have regarding recess. Are the parents pleased with the recess time, materials, and experience?

Internet References

Alliance for Childhood
   http://www.allianceforchildhood.org/

Recess Makes Kids Smarter
   https://www.scholastic.com/teachers/articles/teaching-content/recess-makes-kids-smarter/

Why Kids Need Recess
   http://pathwaystofamilywellness.org/Children-s-Health-Wellness/why-kids-need-recess.html

CATHERINE RAMSTETTER is the founder of Successful Healthy Children, a nonprofit organization focused on school health and wellness. A member of the Ohio chapter of the American Academy of Pediatrics (AAP) Home and School Health Committee, she has researched and written about the importance of recess to children''s development.

ROBERT MURRAY is a professor of human nutrition in the College of Education and Human Ecology at the Ohio State University. A former chair of the Ohio AAP chapter, he was previously a professor in the Department of Pediatrics in the University''s College of Medicine.

Ramstetter, Catherine; Murray, Robert, "Time to Play: Recognizing the Benefits of Recess," *American Educator*, Spring 2017. 17–23. Reprinted by permission of the authors.

Sensory and Art Activities for Infants and Toddlers

Nontoxic material	Nontoxic items to place on or in the material	Surface	Tools	Ages and notes
Tempera paint, foam paint, finger paint	Colored sand and liquid soap	Paper, Plexiglass, wood, cardboard items, natural items, body parts, bubble wrap	Paintbrushes, stamps, sponges, plastic cars, plastic balls	Infants and toddlers
Watercolor block paint or liquid paint	None	Paper, coffee filters	Water, brushes, bottles for liquid watercolor	Toddlers
Contact paper	Colored sand, regular sand, natural materials, paper scraps, pictures from magazines, photos, recycled wrapping paper, pipe cleaners, tissue paper	Table or floor	Scotch tape or similar to affix contact paper to the table	Infants and toddlers
Stickers, tape	None	Paper or skin	None	Infants and toddlers
Construction paper, cardboard, tissue paper, newspaper, butcher paper, etc.	None	Paper can be used as a surface.	Tape to affix to the paper or materials to decorate it	Infants and toddlers Crumpling, tearing, climbing into containers of crumpled paper, and making balls of paper.
Glue	None	Table with trays and paper or cardboard to hold collage	Glue bottles	Toddlers
Playdough, purchased or homemade. (*Note:* Limit how much playdough children eat due to the high salt content or make salt-free playdough, or purchase commercial playdough.)	Colored sand; liquid watercolor, food color, or extract (e.g., vanilla or peppermint); pipe cleaners; Popsicle sticks; leaves, sticks, shells, etc.	Table with trays to define each child's space, or a bin if a group of infants shares the playdough	Cookie cutters, cutting tools, baking tools, ceramic tools, tortilla presses, garlic presses, plastic toys as props	Infants and toddlers
Natural clay	Pipe cleaners, Popsicle sticks, nontoxic branches, water if clay is dry	Table or bin, trays optional	See above	Infants and toddlers Clean up well after using clay to prevent dust buildup.
Water	Liquid watercolor or food color, soap, large ice blocks (but remove when they become smaller), cornstarch (oobleck), wool	Bins on or off a table. Towels taped to floor around this project.	Cups, funnels, bath toys, measuring cups, whisks, items that sink and float, eye droppers for toddlers	Infants and toddlers
Birdseed, sand, soil	Hidden toys or shells under the material. Water in the sand or soil.	Bins inside or outside to decrease mess. Water table.	Containers, sand mills, plastic vehicles or animals. Various sizes of tubes. Plastic beakers.	Infants and toddlers
Nontoxic leaves, pinecones, seedpods, flowers	Water, soil, clay	Table, bin, piles outside	Scissors (for toddlers only)	Infants and toddlers
Stamping ink/dot markers	None	Table with individual papers or butcher paper if this is a communal artwork. Wall with butcher paper.	Stamps for stamp pad. Both age groups are more likely to use hands.	Infants and toddlers

Nontoxic material	Nontoxic items to place on or in the material	Surface	Tools	Ages and notes
Crayons, colored pencils, markers, nontoxic oil pastels, chalk	None	Table with individual papers or butcher paper if this is a communal artwork. Wall with butcher paper.	None	Older infants and toddlers. Use chalk outside or with ventilation to prevent dust buildup.
Fabric	None	Can be connected into a "sensory blanket" with other materials such as bubble wrap for young infants to crawl over. Older children can use it on a table for collage.	Scissors (for toddlers only)	Infants and toddlers Invites open-ended dramatic play and dance for toddlers.

whisks, measuring cups, cupcake tins and wrappers, salt-filled shakers, and other baking tools to the trays. The toddlers jumped right in, making more cakes and cupcakes. They were particularly interested in the salt shakers and sometimes got into conflicts over taking turns using them.

2. We decided to make salt shaker art. We filled small glue bottles with about a tablespoon of glue apiece. We placed construction paper on trays, anticipating glue puddles. We placed colored sand in several recycled spice shakers and taped over some of the holes to make the sand come out slowly. The toddlers made small glue lakes and shook all the sand out into colorful piles. We scooped the excess sand up, refilled the spice containers, and repeated the process. The toddlers did not understand that the glue made the sand stick, or that if they used too much glue the sand would fall off, but they loved the process. As expected, this was a developmentally appropriate outcome. Although children at this age do not carefully use glue, they do enjoy the experience of emptying, squeezing, and making a mess.

3. We added food coloring to the glue in the bottles after observing that the toddlers enjoyed using the glue puddles as paint.

4. The toddlers did not want to stop using shakers—it was so much fun! We took the activity outside to the dramatic play table beside the sandbox. Here the toddlers could make a mess using filled shakers without getting the classroom salty or sandy. They could also refill the shakers with sand. We knew the toddlers would "ruin" the playdough with the sand, but we accepted this as part of the process. This project included the initial playdough and accessories, salt shakers filled with various substances, and glue with and without food color.

Making a Record

To share the children's explorations with parents and visitors to our school, we documented each toddler art/sensory activity in the classroom in a photo essay. "Adventures in the Toddler Room." Here is an excerpt from the toddler room's glue-and-sand activity:

We introduced glue-and-sand painting. This was a direct extension of last week's bakery shop project. We noticed that the toddlers loved using shakers and enjoyed decorating with sand.

Peter is using both hands to squeeze out colored glue from the bottle. He has placed his sand down before the glue. This shows us that he does not understand that the glue will make the sand stick to the paper, but that he is testing out the properties of both materials on the paper.

Andy and Joo are engaging in a similar process, testing the materials without being told how to use them by an adult. They are developing strong fine motor skills as they handle the tools.

Conclusion

We have found that the art and sensory investigations in the infant and toddler classrooms are some of the most exciting that we provide. Well-planned projects that include time for exploration and a way to control—or at least contain—the mess allow everyone to relax and enjoy the process. We encourage you to try art and sensory activities with the infants and toddlers in your care. There is nothing like seeing a child realize that she has caused a mark on a paper, or watching a toddler discover for himself that mixing blue and red makes purple. While art explorations with infants and toddlers are certainly more work for caregivers, they have a strong positive impact on young children's development and learning.

Sources for Art/Sensory Materials

Materials available commercially: Tempera paint, foam paint, watercolor paint, glue, Popsicle sticks, colored sand, paper, contact paper, tape, stamp pads and stamps, bird-seed, feathers, soap, sponges.

Materials found at thrift stores: Cups and funnels, magazines for clipping images for collage, and kitchen utensils.

Nontoxic natural materials (bleach them before children put them in their mouths, using the ratio of bleach to water recommended by your state's licensing protocol): Straw, nontoxic leaves and seeds, flowers and sticks, wool, shells, rocks, gourds, pinecones, sand, mud.

Using these materials is beneficial to young children—handling nontoxic pinecones and leaves in a bin encourages a love of nature and engages all of a child's senses (White & Stoecklin 2008).

Materials found in the home or classroom: Paper towel/toilet paper rolls, yogurt containers, plastic water bottles, recycled paper, newspaper, cardboard boxes of all sizes, egg cartons, canning jar lids, water, old towels to make rags.

Materials created from scratch: Playdough, finger paint, oobleck, "clean mud," colored salt/sand. There are many recipes for these online and in the library.

References

Arnwine, B. 2007. *Starting Sensory Integration Therapy: Fun Activities That Won't Destroy Your Home or Classroom.* Arlington, TX: Future Horizons.

Cryer, D., T. Harms, & C. Riley. 2004. *All about the ITERS-R.* Lewisville, NC: Pact House.

Curtis, D. & M. Carter. 1996. *Reflecting Children's Lives: A Handbook for Planning Child-Centered Curriculum.* Saint Paul, MN: Redleaf.

Derman-Sparks, L., & J. Olsen Edwards. 2010. *Anti-Bias Education for Young Children and Ourselves.* Washington, DC: NAEYC.

Goldhawk, S. 1998. *Young Children and the Arts: Making Creative Connections. A Report of the Task Force on Children's Learning and the Arts, Birth to Age Eight.* Washington, DC: The Arts Education Partnership. www.eric.ed.gov./PDFS/ED453968.pdf.

Harms, T., R.M. Clifford, & D. Cryer. 2005. *Early Childhood Environment Rating Scale Revised.* New York: Teachers College Press.

Harms, T., D. Cryer, & R.M. Clifford. 2007. *Infant/Toddler Environment Rating Scale Revised Edition.* New York: Teachers College Press.

Miller, K. 1999. *Simple Steps: Developmental Activities for Infants, Toddlers, and Two-Year-Olds.* Beltsville, MD: Gryphon House.

Smith, D., & J. Goldhaber. 2004. *Poking, Pinching and Pretending: Documenting Toddlers' Explorations with Clay.* Saint Paul, MN: Redleaf.

White, R., & V.L. Stoecklin. 2008. "Nurturing Children's Biophilia: Developmentally Appropriate Environmental Education for Young Children." *Collage: Resources for Early Childhood Educators,* Nov. www.whitehutchinson.com/children/articles/nurturing.shtml.

Critical Thinking

1. Write a culturally sensitive policy on the use of food products in your classroom.
2. Choose two of the materials listed on the chart of sensory and art activities in the article and extend and develop an activity that you could use with infants and toddlers.

Internet References

Idea Box
http://theideabox.com

Make Your Own Webpage
www.teacherweb.com

Meet Me at the Corner
www.meetmeatthecorner.org

Teacher Planet
http://teacherplanet.com

Teacher Quick Source
www.teacherquicksource.com

Teachers Helping Teachers
www.pacificnet.net/~mandel

Zero to Three
zerotothree.org

TRUDI SCHWARZ, MS, is the infant room head teacher at the University of California–Davis Center for Child and Family Studies' NAEYC-Accredited Early Childhood Lab School. She has presented at California AEYC and local early childhood education conferences. Her professional interests include infant language development and creating innovative infant curricula. tkschwarz@ucdavis.edu.

JULIA LUCKENBILL, MA, is the infant and toddler program coordinator for the Early Childhood Lab School at UC–Davis. She has directed several preschool programs in California. In addition to her classroom and lecture responsibilities at the school, she presents on a range of child development topics for parents, teachers, and students. Her interests include sensory activities and integrating Reggio Emilia philosophy into US schools. jaluckenbill@ucdavis.edu.

Article   Prepared by: Karen Menke Paciorek, *Eastern Michigan University*

Time for Play

A new movement of parents and childhood experts want to save an endangered human behavior: joyful, spontaneous play unaided by electronic screens and hovering parents.

STEPHANIE HANES

Learning Outcomes

After reading this article, you will be able to:

- Chronicle how play has evolved over the past half century.

- Explain to administrators and families why play should be an integral part of the curriculum.

Havely Taylor knows that her two children do not play the way she did when she was growing up.

When Ms. Taylor was a girl, in a leafy suburb of Birmingham, Ala., she climbed trees, played imaginary games with her friends, and transformed a hammock into a storm-tossed sea vessel. She even whittled bows and arrows from downed branches around the yard and had "wars" with friends—something she admits she'd probably freak out about if her children did it today.

"I mean, you could put an eye out like that," she says with a laugh.

Her children—Ava, age 12, and Henry, 8—have had a different experience. They live in Baltimore, where Taylor works as an art teacher. Between school, homework, violin lessons, ice-skating, theater, and play dates, there is little time for the sort of freestyle play Taylor remembers. Besides, Taylor says, they live in the city, with a postage stamp of a backyard and the ever-present threat of urban danger.

"I was kind of afraid to let them go out unsupervised in Baltimore . . . ," she says, of how she started down this path with the kids. "I'm really a protective mom. There wasn't much playing outside."

This difference has always bothered her, she says, because she believes that play is critical for children's developing emotions, creativity, and intelligence. But when she learned that her daughter's middle school had done away with recess, and even free time after lunch, she decided to start fighting for play.

"It seemed almost cruel," she says. "Play is important for children—it's something so obvious it's almost hard to articulate. How can you talk about childhood without talking about play? It's almost as if they are trying to get rid of childhood."

Taylor joined a group of parents pressuring the principal to let their children have a recess, citing experts such as the US Centers for Disease Control and Prevention, which recommends that all students have at least 60 minutes of physical activity every day. They issued petitions and held meetings. And although the school has not yet agreed to change its curriculum, Taylor says she feels their message is getting more recognition.

She is not alone in her concerns. In recent years, child development experts, parents, and scientists have been sounding an increasingly urgent alarm about the decreasing amount of time that children—and adults, for that matter—spend playing. A combination of social forces, from a No Child Left Behind focus on test scores to the push for children to get ahead with programmed extracurricular activities, leaves less time for the roughhousing, fantasizing, and pretend worlds advocates say are crucial for development.

Meanwhile, technology and a wide-scale change in toys have shifted what happens when children do engage in leisure activity, in a way many experts say undermines long-term emotional and intellectual abilities. An 8-year-old today, for instance, is more likely to be playing with a toy that has a computer chip, or attending a tightly supervised soccer practice, than making up an imaginary game with friends in the backyard or street.

But play is making a comeback. Bolstered by a growing body of scientific research detailing the cognitive benefits of different types of play, parents such as Taylor are pressuring school administrations to bring back recess and are fighting against a trend to move standardized testing and increased academic instruction to kindergarten.

Public officials are getting in on the effort. First lady Michelle Obama and US Secretary of Education Arne Duncan, for instance, have made a push for playgrounds nationwide. Local politicians from Baltimore to New York have participated in events such as the Ultimate Block Party—a metropolitan-wide play gathering. Meanwhile, business and corporate groups, worried about a future workforce hampered by a lack of creativity and innovation, support the effort.

"It's at a tipping point," says Susan Magsamen, the director of Interdisciplinary Partnerships at the Johns Hopkins University School of Medicine Brain Science Institute, who has headed numerous child play efforts. "Parents are really anxious and really overextended. Teachers are feeling that way, too."

So when researchers say and can show that "it's OK to not be so scheduled [and] programmed—that time for a child to daydream is a good thing," Ms. Magsamen says, it confirms what families and educators "already knew, deep down, but didn't have the permission to act upon."

But play, it seems, isn't that simple.

Scientists disagree about what sort of play is most important, government is loath to regulate the type of toys and technology that increasingly shape the play experience, and parents still feel pressure to supervise children's play rather than let them go off on their own. (Nearly two-thirds of Americans in a December *Monitor* TIPP poll, for instance, said it is irresponsible to let children play without supervision; almost as many said studying is more important than play.) And there is still pressure on schools to sacrifice playtime—often categorized as frivolous—in favor of lessons that boost standardized test scores.

"Play is still terribly threatened," says Susan Linn, an instructor of psychiatry at Harvard Medical School and director of the nonprofit Campaign for a Commercial-Free Childhood. But, she adds, "what is changing is that there's a growing recognition that the erosion of play may be a problem . . . we need to do something about."

One could say that the state of play, then, is at a crossroads. What happens to it—how it ends up fitting into American culture, who defines it, what it looks like—will have long-term implications for childhood, say those who study it.

Some go even further: The future of play will define society overall and even determine the future of our species.

"Play is the fundamental equation that makes us human," says Stuart Brown, the founder of the California-based National Institute for Play. "Its absence, in my opinion, is pathology."

Can You Define "Play"?

But before advocates can launch a defense of play, they need to grapple with a surprisingly difficult question. What, exactly, is play?

It might seem obvious. Parents know when their children are playing, whether it's a toddler scribbling on a piece of paper, an infant shaking a rattle, or a pair of 10-year-olds dressing up and pretending to be superheroes.

But even Merriam-Webster's Collegiate Dictionary definition, "recreational activity; especially the spontaneous action of children," is often inaccurate, according to scientists and child development researchers. Play for children is neither simply recreational nor necessarily spontaneous, they say.

"Play is when children are using something they've learned, to try it out and see how it works, to use it in new ways—it's problem solving and enjoying the satisfaction of problems

Evolution of Play

1950s:
- **Outdoor play** without adult supervision was common in both urban and rural US settings.
- **Different ages** played together.
- **Bicycles and balls** were the main outdoor toys, and board games were the most common inside.
- **Much of play** revolved around traditional games such as baseball, modified to fit space and materials.

1980s:
- **Use of toys increased,** and many were 'branded'— connected to TV characters—Barbies, Power Rangers, My Little Ponies, etc.
- **Outdoor play** was likely to be adult-supervised or part of an 'organized activity.'
- **TV viewing** was increasingly a part of free time.
- **Athletics become more formal** and age-based— such as soccer camp for 7-year-olds rather than neighborhood pickup soccer in a vacant lot.

2010s:
- **Toys are the center** of play; most are connected to media characters and are somehow electronic.
- **Most free time** is screen time spent in front of the TV, computer, etc.
- **Unsupervised outdoor time** is almost nonexistent. Physical activity of any kind has decreased.
- **Multi-age,** cross-gender play is disappearing, even among siblings.

—Stephanie Hanes

solv[ed]," says Diane Levin, a professor of education at Wheelock College in Boston. But Ms. Levin says that, in her class on the meaning and development of play, she never introduces one set definition.

"This is something that people argue about," she says.

Scientists and child advocates agree that there are many forms of play. There is "attunement play," the sort of interaction where a mother and infant might gaze at each other and babble back and forth. There is "object play," where a person might manipulate a toy such as a set of marbles; "rough and tumble play"; and "imaginative play." "Free play" is often described as kids playing on their own, without any adult supervision; "guided play" is when a child or other player takes the lead, but a mentor is around to, say, help facilitate the LEGO castle construction.

But often, says Dr. Brown at the National Institute for Play, a lot is happening all at once. He cites the time he tried to do a brain scan of his then-4-year-old grandson at play with his stuffed tiger.

"He was clearly playing," Brown recalls.

"And then he says to me, 'Grandpa, what does the tiger say?' I say, 'Roar!' And then he says, 'No, it says, "Moo!"' and then laughs like crazy. How are you going to track *that*? He's pretending, he's making a joke, he's interacting."

This is one reason Brown says play has been discounted—both culturally and, until relatively recently, within the academic community, where detractors argue that play is so complex it cannot be considered one specific behavior, that it is an amalgamation of many different acts. These scientists—known as "play skeptics"—don't believe play can be responsible for all sorts of positive effects, in part because play itself is suspect.

"It is so difficult to define and objectify," Brown notes.

But most researchers agree that play clearly exists, even if it can't always be coded in the standard scientific way of other

A 2-Year-Old's Dilemma: Angry Birds or Plain Old Blocks?

The Games Kids No Longer Play

Once upon a time, a typical gift for a child was a set of blocks. Plain old blocks with no batteries or screens, no electronic voice asking to be friends, no game of Angry Birds somehow embedded in their cubic walls.

No longer.

As anyone who braved toy stores this past holiday season knows, the bulk of gear for children these days is far more technologically decked out, with everything from flashing lights to 3-D computer screens to disembodied voices. And this, say child development experts, is turning into a massive problem.

High-stimuli toys, even many of those advertised as "educational" or "interactive," actually serve to diminish children's creativity, many experts say. Instead of using their minds to imagine how to use a toy—how to build a castle with blocks, say—they simply push a button or watch a flashing light. The toy is doing the work, which is the reverse of what researchers say is ideal.

"The best toy is 90 percent child and 10 percent toy," says Susan Linn, a Harvard University psychiatry instructor and cofounder of the Campaign for a Commercial-Free Childhood. "The [perfect] toy's meaning and its use changes at the child's behest."

At the same time, a large percentage of children's toys are based on media characters—Transformers, for instance, were top sellers this past holiday season. The problem with this, says Diane Levin, an education professor at Wheelock College in Boston, is that when a child plays with a toy that already has a character description, the play tends to be limited; the child doesn't invent the figure's personality or actions because those characteristics are already determined.

"Play material is very important," Ms. Levin says. "When they have something that is just something they saw on TV, they will use it the same way. They will imitate."

And of course, there is the issue of screen time. According to the Kaiser Family Foundation, 8-to-18-year-olds now spend 7.5 hours a day in front of one or more screens. This, according to the American Academy of Pediatrics, is too much. It recommends no screen time for children 2 years old and younger, and no more than two hours a day for older ones.

But some top-selling toys this past season—including infant toys—were screen-based. (Teachers Resisting Unhealthy Children's Entertainment named a tablet computer for babies the worst toy of the year; a similar device was in the Toys "R" Us Top 15 Christmas gifts for 2011.)

Many of these screen toys advertise themselves as educational, tapping into parents' desire to help children get ahead in a technologically focused world. In a December *Monitor* TIPP poll, for instance, two-thirds of Americans agreed with the statement "the earlier a child can use technology, the better off he or she will be." Yet numerous studies have found no educational benefit—and possibly some harm—in early screen time.

It comes down, child advocates say, to money.

"One of the reasons that creative play has been diminishing in the United States is that it's not lucrative," Dr. Linn says. "Companies make less money when children play creatively. Children who play creatively need less stuff, and they can use the same thing over and over again—mud, water, blocks, dolls that don't do anything."

—Stephanie Hanes

human behaviors. And the importance of play, Brown and others say, is huge.

Brown became interested in play as a young clinical psychiatrist when he was researching, somewhat incongruously, mass murderers. Although he concluded that many factors contributed to the psychosis of his subjects, Brown noticed that a common denominator was that none had participated in standard play behavior as children, such as interacting positively with parents or engaging in games with other children. As he continued his career, he took "play histories" of patients, eventually recording 6,000. He saw a direct correlation between play behavior and happiness, from childhood into adulthood.

It has a lot to do with joy, he says: "In the play studies I'd find many adults who had a pretty playful childhood but then confined themselves to grinding, to always being responsible, always seeing just the next task. [They] are less flexible and have a chronic, smoldering depression. That lack of joyfulness gets to you."

Brown later worked with ethologists—scientists who study animal behavior—to observe how other species, from honeybees to Labrador retrievers, play. This behavior in a variety of species is sophisticated—from "self-handicapping," so a big dog plays fairly with a small dog, to cross-species play, such as a polar bear romping with a sled dog. He also studied research on play depravation, noting how rat brains change negatively when they are deprived of some sorts of play.

Brown became convinced that human play—for adults as well as children—is not only joyful but necessary, a behavior that has survived despite connections in some studies to injury and danger (for example, animals continue to play even though they're likely to be hunted while doing so) and is connected to the most ancient part of human biology.

'Executive' Play

Other scientists are focusing on the specific impacts of play. In a small, brick testing room next to the "construction zone" at the Boston Children's Museum, for instance, Daniel Friel sits with a collection of brightly colored tubing glued to a board. The manager of the Early Childhood Cognition Lab in the Department of Brain and Cognitive Sciences at the Massachusetts Institute of Technology (MIT), he observes children at play with puppets and squeaky toys, rubber balls and fabulously created pipe sculptures. Depending on the experiment, Mr. Friel and other researchers record such data as the time a child plays with a particular object or what color ball is picked out of a container. These observations lead to insights on how children form their understanding of the world.

"We are interested in exploratory play, how kids develop cause and effect, how they use evidence," he says.

The collection of tubing, for instance, is part of a study designed by researcher Elizabeth Bonawitz and tests whether the way an object is presented can limit a child's exploration. If a teacher introduces the toy, which has a number of hidden points of interest—a mirror, a button that lights up, etc.—but tells a child about only one feature, the child is less likely to discover everything the toy can do than a child who receives the toy from a teacher who feigns ignorance. Without limiting instruction from an adult, it seems, a child is far more creative. In other words, adult hovering and instruction, from how to play soccer to how to build the best LEGO city, can be limiting.

Taken together, the MIT experiments show children calculating probabilities during play, developing assumptions about their physical environment, and adjusting perceptions according to the direction of authority figures. Other researchers are also discovering a breathtaking depth to play: how it develops chronological awareness and its link to language development and self-control.

The latter point has been a hot topic recently. Self-regulation—the buzzword here is "executive function," referring to abilities such as planning, multitasking, and reasoning—may be more indicative of future academic success than IQ, standardized tests, or other assessments, according to a host of recent studies from institutions such as Pennsylvania State University and the University of British Columbia.

Curriculums that boost executive function have become increasingly popular. Two years ago, Elizabeth Billings-Fouhy, director of the public Children's Place preschool in Lexington, Mass., decided to adopt one such program, called Tools of the Mind. It was created by a pair of child development experts—Deborah Leong and Elena Bodrova—in the early 1990s after a study evaluating federal early literacy efforts found no positive outcomes.

"People started saying there must be something else," Dr. Leong says. "And we believed what was missing was self-regulation and executive function."

She became interested in a body of research from Russia that showed children who played more had better self-regulation. This made sense to her, she says. For example, studies have shown that children can stand still far longer if they are playing soldier; games such as Simon says depend on concentration and rule-following.

"Play is when kids regulate their behavior voluntarily," Leong says. Eventually, she and Dr. Bodrova developed the curriculum used in the Children's Place today, where students spend the day in different sorts of play. They act out long-form make-believe scenes, they build their own props, and they participate in buddy reading, where one child has a picture of a pair of lips and the other has a picture of ears. The child with the lips reads; the other listens. Together, these various play exercises increase self-control, educators say.

This was on clear display recently at the Children's Place. Nearly half the children there have been labeled as special needs students with everything from autism to physical limitations. The others are mainstream preschoolers—an "easier" group, perhaps, but still not one typically renowned for its self-control.

But in a brightly colored classroom, a group of 3-, 4-, and 5-year-olds are notably calm; polite and quiet, sitting in pairs, taking turns "reading" a picture book.

"Here are scissors, a brush. . .," a boy named Aiden points out to his partner, Kyle, who is leaning in attentively.

"Oh, don't forget the paint," Kyle says, although he's mostly quiet, as it's his turn to listen.

Aiden nods and smiles: "Yes, the paint."

When Aiden is finished, the boys switch roles. Around them, another dozen toddlers do the same—all without teacher direction. The Tools classrooms have the reputation of being far better-behaved than mainstream classes.

"We have been blown away," says Ms. Billings-Fouhy, the director, comparing how students are doing now versus before the Tools curriculum. "We can't believe the difference."

Educators and scientists have published overwhelmingly positive analyses since the early 2000s of the sort of curriculum Tools of the Mind employs. But recently the popularity of the play-based curriculum has skyrocketed, with more preschools adopting the Tools method and parenting chat rooms buzzing about the curriculum. Two years ago, for instance, Billings-Fouhy had to convince people about changing the Children's Place program. Now out-of-district parents call to get their children in.

> **"Play is the fundamental equation that makes us human. Its absence, in my opinion, is pathology."**
>
> —Stuart Brown, founder of the National Institute for Play

"I think we're at this place where everyone is coming to the conclusion that play is important," Leong says. "Not just because of self-regulation, but because people are worried about the development of the whole child—their social and emotional development as well."

Today's Kids Don't Know How to Play

But not all play is created equal, experts warn.

The Tools of the Mind curriculum, for instance, uses what Leong calls "intentional mature play"—play that is facilitated and guided by trained educators. If children in the class were told to simply go and play, she says, the result probably would be a combination of confusion, mayhem, and paralysis.

"People say, 'Let's bring back play,'" Leong says. "But they don't realize play won't just appear spontaneously, especially not in preschool. . . . The culture of childhood itself has changed."

For a host of reasons, today's children do not engage in all sorts of developmentally important play that prior generations automatically did. In her class at Wheelock College, Levin has students interview people over the age of 50 about how they played. In the 1950s and '60s, students regularly find, children played outdoors no matter where they lived, and without parental supervision. They played sports but adjusted the rules to fit the space and material—a goal in soccer, for instance, might be kicking a tennis ball to the right of the trash can. They had few toys, and older children tended to act as "play mentors" to younger children, instructing them in the ways of make-believe games.

That has changed dramatically, she says. In the early 1980s, the federal government deregulated children's advertising, allowing TV shows to essentially become half-hour-long advertisements for toys such as Power Rangers, My Little Ponies, and Teenage Mutant Ninja Turtles. Levin says that's when children's play changed. They wanted specific toys, to use them in the specific way that the toys appeared on TV.

Today, she says, children are "second generation deregulation," and not only have more toys—mostly media-based—but also lots of screens. A Kaiser Family Foundation study recently found that 8-to-18-year-olds spend an average of 7.5 hours in front of a screen every day, with many of those hours involving multiscreen multitasking. Toys for younger children tend to have reaction-based operations, such as push-buttons and flashing lights.

Take away the gadgets and the media-based scripts, Levin and others say, and many children today simply don't know what to do.

"If they don't have the toys, they don't know how to play," she says.

The American educational system, increasingly teaching to standardized tests, has also diminished children's creativity, says Kathy Hirsh-Pasek, a professor of psychology and director

childhood settings. Block play offers essential opportunities for promoting children's social and emotional development. Through building together, children learn to share, take turns, and collaborate in meaningful ways. In addition, construction play provides opportunities for children to learn problem solving, math, science, and language skills.

Math Concepts

Pratt designed unit blocks with a standard proportion in mind to promote children's understanding of mathematical relationships. As children manipulate the blocks, they develop a deeper cognitive understanding of the relationships between objects. This type of learning is known as *logico-mathematical knowledge* (Kamii 1990), and it enables children to master skills such as counting, sorting, classifying, and identifying shapes. These skills form the foundation on which mathematical processes are learned. Chalufour and Worth (2004) suggest these specific strategies for promoting math skills in the block center:

- Count and record the number of blocks used to build a tower.
- Measure the height of a structure using measuring tools such as measuring tape, string, or Unifix cubes (small interlocking cubes used to teach measurement).
- Encourage descriptions of structures using mathematical attributes such as shape, number, size, and order.

Science Constructs

Children can learn scientific constructs such as height, gravity, balance, action/reaction, and cause and effect through block play. Children can make further discoveries as they experiment with cardboard tubes, lengths of PVC pipe, straws, string, small boxes, table tennis balls, and toy cars. Provide a variety of surfaces for children to build on, such as tile, cardboard, sponges, bubble wrap, and carpet squares (Giles & Tunks 2013). Guiding children by asking open-ended questions as they experiment opens the door for further discoveries. For example, "What can you use to connect these two blocks?" or "What would happen if you tried to balance a block on top?"

Language Skills

Opportunities for using language and increasing vocabulary are an authentic outcome of block play. Children engage in conversations with each other during block play (Chalufour & Worth 2004). They negotiate ideas as they build cooperatively and, once a structure is complete, might role-play with the block structure as the center for their play (Wellhousen & Keiff 2001). For example, following a field trip to a firehouse, three children construct a fire station from unit blocks. They

Additional Contemporary Construction Materials

Block Type	Features
Mega Bloks First Builders (ages 1–5 years)	• Large size of blocks make it easy for small hands to grasp • Bright, primary colors • Easy to stack
DUPLOs (ages 18 months to 5 years)	• Slightly larger than LEGOs • Easier for young children to put together and pull apart
Waffle blocks (ages 2–4 years)	• Waffle-shaped plastic pieces that snap together • Bright colors in various sizes
Cardboard blocks (ages 2–6)	• Lightweight, easy to stack • Crush resistant • Sets include varied sizes and colors
Bristle blocks (ages 2 and up)	• Soft, flexible interlocking plastic bristles are used to connect blocks • Can be attached to 6" × 7" building plate • Bright colors
Foam building blocks (ages 2 and up)	• Multicolored blocks in various shapes and sizes • Chunky foam pieces are easy to grip
Large interlocking blocks (ages 2 and up)	• Flexible plastic pieces in four shapes • Rectangular shape measures 4.5" × 9" • Durable and washable
Soft unit blocks (ages 2 and up)	• Built to the same scale as unit blocks • Made of dense foam • Lightweight, colorful, and safe if thrown
Building bricks (ages 3 and up)	• 2" plastic cubes that snap together • Made of bright, colorful plastic
Large hollow blocks (ages 3 and up)	• Wooden blocks • Used to make child-size structures such as forts • Five different sizes and shapes, plus boards
Tabletop building blocks (ages 3 and up)	• Variety of shapes • Smaller version of unit blocks • May be natural wood or wood painted bright colors
LEGOs (ages 4 and up)	• Bright colors • Small, interlocking pieces • Require fine motor skills

share ideas about adding accessories, including a toy fire truck, a plastic dalmatian, and a piece of surgical tubing that serves as a fire hose. They adjust the size of the fire station to accommodate the fire truck. Once complete, they put on plastic firefighter hats and become firefighters. Imagination and language energizes their play. Next, they build a house from spare blocks so they can rush into action to save lives and put out fires.

Conclusion

Thanks to Caroline Pratt and the many early childhood educators who followed, unit blocks have enjoyed a long and rich history in early childhood education. They have stood the test of time and the ever-evolving philosophy and approaches in early childhood education. Generations of young children have explored and learned through playing with unit blocks over the past century, and there is little doubt that playing with unit blocks will continue to be a favorite activity among young children for the next 100 years!

References

Brosterman, N. 1997. *Inventing Kindergarten.* New York: Abrams.

Chalufour, I., & K. Worth. 2004. *Building Structures With Young Children.* St. Paul, MN: Redleaf.

Epstein, A.S., L.J. Schweinhart, & L. McAdoo. 1996. *Models of Early Childhood Education.* Ypsilanti, MI: HighScope.

Fowlkes, M.A. 1984. "Gifts From Childhood's Godmother: Patty Smith Hill." *Childhood Education* 61 (1): 44–49.

Giles, R., & K. Tunks. 2013. "Building Young Scientists: Developing Scientific Literacy Through Construction Play." *Early Years: Journal of the Texas Association for the Education of Young Children* 34 (2): 22–27.

Helfrich, M.S. 2011. *Montessori Learning in the 21st Century: A Guide for Parents and Teachers.* Troutdale, OR: NewSage.

Hinitz, B.F. 2013. "History of Early Childhood Education in Multicultural Perspective." Chap. 1 in *Approaches to Early Childhood Education,* 6th ed., eds. J. Roopnarine & J.E. Johnson, 3–33. Boston: Pearson.

Hirsch, E.S., ed. 1996. *The Block Book.* 3rd ed. Washington, DC: NAEYC.

Kamii, C. 1990. "Constructivism and Beginning Arithmetic (K–2)." In *Teaching and Learning Mathematics in the 1990s: 1990 Yearbook,* eds. T.J. Cooney & C.R. Hirsch, 22–30. Reston, VA: National Council of Teachers of Mathematics.

Kilpatrick, W.H. 1914. *The Montessori System Examined.* New York: Houghton Mifflin. http://archive.org/details/montessorisystem00kilprich

Leeb-Lundberg, K. 1996. "The Block Builder Mathematician." In E.S. Hirsch, 30–51.

Montessori, M. [1912] 1964. *The Montessori Method.* Trans. A.E. George. New York: Stokes. http://digital.library.upenn.edu/women/montessori/method/method.html

Morgan, H. 2011. *Early Childhood Education: History, Theory, and Practice.* 2nd ed. New York, NY: Rowman & Littlefield.

Snyder, A. 1972. *Dauntless Women in Childhood Education, 1856–1931.* Washington, DC: Association for Childhood Education International

Tunks, K.W. 2009. "Block Play: Practical Suggestions for Common Dilemmas." *Dimensions of Early Childhood* 37 (1): 3–8.

Wellhousen, K., & J. Kieff. 2001. *A Constructivist Approach to Block Play in Early Childhood.* Stamford, CT: Cengage.

Wiggin, K.D., & N.A. Smith. [1895] 2010. *The Republic of Childhood: Froebel's Gifts.* New York: Houghton Mifflin. http://archive.org/details/froebelsgifts00wiggrich

Critical Thinking

1. If your administrator gave you $1,000 to purchase blocks for your preschool classroom, what would you buy and why? You may use the internet references below to assist you in developing the list of materials.

2. How have blocks and block play changed over the 100+ years they have been available for young children?

3. Write a one paragraph note to the families of children in your kindergarten class describing why you have blocks in the kindergarten room and what their children will learn from block play.

Internet References

City and Country School Blocks
    http://www.cityandcountry.org/page/Programs/Blocks-Program
Community Play Things
    http://www.communityplaythings.com/products/blocks
Early Childhood News
    http://www.earlychildhoodnews.com/earlychildhood/article_view.aspx?ArticleID=397
Play and Playground Encyclopedia
    http://www.playgroundprofessionals.com/b/block-play

KARYN W. TUNKS, PhD, is an associate professor of education at the University of South Alabama, in Mobile. She has published widely on the topic of block play and is the coauthor of the book *A Constructivist Approach to Block Play in Early, Childhood.*

Tunks, Karyn W. From *Young Children,* vol. 68, no. 5, November 2013, 82–87. Copyright ©2013 by National Association for the Education of Young Children. Used with permission.

Article   Prepared by: Karen Menke Paciorek, *Eastern Michigan University*

Animal Attraction: Including Animals in Early Childhood Classrooms

CLARISSA M. UTTLEY

Learning Outcomes

After reading this article, you will be able to:

- Advocate to acquire an animal for your classroom or your child's classroom.

- Describe the benefits for children when they have an animal in their classroom.

- List the pros and cons of having a classroom animal.

Animals and children have been intricately connected throughout history. Some parents bring home a pet to help their children gain a sense of responsibility and to encourage social-emotional development. Children learn to care for others, increase their ability to empathize, and gain self-esteem as they care for pets. Early childhood educators recognize the benefits of including animals in the classroom to address the developmental and educational goals of the children they teach.

Educators use a variety of strategies to include animals in support of the curriculum. They maintain classroom pets as permanent residents, welcome family pets for short visits, host guest visitors from local zoos or farms, and schedule field trips to environmental education facilities. Teachers have included animals in programs to encourage children to read (Shaw 2013), increase environmental stewardship (Bailie 2010; Torquati et al. 2010), support cultural education (Dubosarsky et al. 2011), enhance curriculum goals (Gee et al. 2012; Hachey & Butler 2012), and address challenging behaviors (Nielson & Delude 1989; Wedl & Kotrschal 2009).

A Survey of Animals in the Classroom

There is limited research on the numbers and types of animals found in early childhood classrooms, so I conducted a study to examine early childhood educators' use of animals in their classrooms. This article presents survey results describing the types of animals included in respondents' programs. It offers practical strategies to help educators decide whether to include animals in the classroom, select the right animals, engage children with animals to support learning goals, and assess whether the children and animals are benefitting from these experiences. The article provides examples from my own experiences and from the experiences of study participants.

More than 1,400 NAEYC-accredited programs for young children, with classrooms for birth through third grade, participated in the study. (Some birth-through-kindergarten NAEYC-accredited programs have after-school or older classrooms as extra components.) Nearly two-thirds (879) of the participants reported having animals in their classrooms.

There are many types of animals in these classrooms. Fish are by far the most common—approximately 50 percent. Watching fish can reduce blood pressure and ease anxiety, especially when used in a medical office (Jackson 2012). Fish can be extremely beneficial in educational settings too. Several participants mentioned how easy it is to care for fish and how well children react to seeing these colorful creatures.

A lead teacher in a preschool classroom in Washington, DC, says,

We have a variety of fish swimming happily in the tank. We have black lace angel fish, moonlight gouramis, gold tetras, sucker fish, and salt and pepper catfish. The children *love* them! There is only one sucker fish, so whenever they spot it they get very excited. There is a bench around the tank so the children can hang out there whenever they're feeling out of sorts.

Amphibians and reptiles are also well represented in the study. Teachers use frogs, toads, and lizards to support educational activities and to ease classroom transitions. Animals can change the classroom environment and engage children in ways many children have not previously experienced. Classroom pets can be the support that some children need and a vehicle for educators to use in reaching children with challenging behaviors.

Serious Considerations for Teachers

There are some important points to consider before bringing animals into an early childhood classroom. First, think about your own comfort level with animals and your knowledge of how to care for specific animals. According to the study, educators who have had positive experiences with their own pets are more likely to include animals in the classroom. More than 67 percent of respondents who have classroom pets also have pets at home. One center director in Georgia emphasized the importance for educators of being familiar with the needs of any animal in the classroom to prevent its inadvertent mistreatment. Having seen such cases, she feels strongly that "in centers where we have animals, it is of primary importance that the teacher has actually cared for a pet before."

Second, carefully articulate and examine the intended educational and developmental outcomes. Remember that multiple lives (animals' and people's) are affected when keeping classroom pets, so it is essential to give careful thought to how to safely and appropriately include animals in the curriculum.

For example, a first grade teacher at a university-based early care and education program in California wanted to extend the university's focus on environmental sustainability to his classroom curriculum. To help the children learn how they and their families could set up compost piles at home, he writes that he "created a worm farm that was used daily to recycle snack food wastes (peels, leftovers, and such). Caring for this farm (and learning about recycling) has become an important part of the class routine." Working with invertebrates was an appropriate choice to meet the curriculum's educational goals.

Discuss the financial resources available to care for an animal well before deciding whether to acquire classroom pets or which type to include.

And third, be mindful of the resources necessary for keeping any kind of animal in the classroom. As many study participants noted, financial and space resources are limited in most early childhood classrooms, and adding animals to the environment may further strain the budget. Costs can include veterinarian expenses, housing and food supplies, and materials to support the healthy development of the animals. One respondent, a kindergarten teacher in Colorado, shares that "because of our economy and a reduced budget, we have limited our classroom pets to hermit crabs. Typically, we also have fancy mice; however, the cost of appropriate materials, such as bedding, has prevented us from acquiring new mice." Discuss the financial resources available to care for an animal well before deciding whether to acquire classroom pets or which type to include.

More Considerations and Challenges

In addition to the considerations regarding personal experiences with pets, the animal—curriculum connections, and the potential strain on the budget, there are a few other points that respondents expressed as concerns.

Animal Well-Being

Animals have certain needs in terms of natural light, heat, privacy, and so on. To meet those needs and ensure that an animal feels as comfortable as possible, establish an area of the room specifically for the pet. Consider the placement of the animal's enclosure and how the children will engage with it. An adult must be able to easily view the children's interactions with both the animal and the enclosure. A case in point from a teacher in Nevada:

> When we first introduced an aquarium to a toddler classroom, a new child, on his first day, broke the front of the aquarium with a wooden truck. We had water and fish everywhere! Fortunately, there was an aquarium in the next class, so all the fish survived.

> The teachable moment was explaining to children how fish need water to live and breathe; it also gave us a chance to go over classroom rules and how trucks work better on the floor instead of in the air. We replaced the aquarium, and children still enjoy watching the fish.

Lifespan

Remember that animals are living beings, and as such they have a lifespan. Thoughtfulness in preparing for a pet's end-of-life care is important. This includes a plan to deal with any common illnesses that a particular animal species tends to contract (for example, rats typically grow tumors, fish commonly get ich [*Ichthyophthirius multifiliis*]). It also involves thinking about ways to discuss the death of a pet with the children and their families.

Several educators reported that although discussing the death of a classroom pet was not a welcome experience, they felt that being honest with the children and their families about life cycles helped some children deal with their relatives' deaths. A touching story provided by a center director from New Hampshire describes the class's experience with the death of their classroom pet:

> Last year we had a rabbit in our 4-year-olds class. Unfortunately, the rabbit died halfway through the school year. We were all sad, but realized that his death helped some children open up to us and to their parents about their fear of dying or losing a loved one. One child spoke for the first time about her mom being sick with cancer.
>
> The rabbit's death was an experience that allowed us all to show our true emotions. Some parents said their children cried at home; some children prayed for the rabbit and some children saw him happily hopping in their dreams! We shared books about dying with the children—one being *All Dogs Go To Heaven*—and the teacher changed the wording to fit the rabbit.

Ethics

Even center directors and educators who see the value of including animals in early childhood classrooms raise major concerns regarding the ethics of keeping animals in classrooms. Study participants expressed worries about issues such as finding the time to properly care for the animal, acquiring enough knowledge to be responsible for the animal, and maintaining a high level of engagement between the children and the animal so the animal does not get abandoned or become just another piece of furniture.

Be aware of times when animals are stressed, and the possible reasons for the stress. A stressed animal is likely to behave differently and to become ill (Fine 2010). To maintain a safe and engaging classroom for both children and animals, learn what is necessary to maintain animals' emotional well-being.

Think also about the experiences of families' and staff's pets that visit the classroom. Pets that enjoy visiting the early childhood classroom get excited about their "work" and have been known to display behaviors that indicate they anticipate these visits. For example, my dog, Nina, gets excited when I take her working vest out of the closet; she seems to understand we are going to visit children. She runs to the door with her tail wagging and eagerly jumps into the backseat of the car. If or when the visits cease, it is common for the pets to experience depression (Kwong & Bartholomew 2011). Animal caregivers need to be aware of the psychological impacts, both positive and negative, that classroom visits may have on the pets.

Health and Hygiene

It is very important for children and educators to use proper hygiene when interacting with animals of any type. All who touch an animal or its food, bedding, or enclosure should wash their hands immediately after the encounter. The animal enclosure should be well maintained and cleaned regularly by an adult. Proper disposal of animal waste ensures a healthy classroom environment for the children and the animal.

Check national accreditation standards and state licensing guidelines, and consult with veterinarians and other animal specialists, when selecting classroom pets. Large-beaked birds can inflict serious injury to tiny fingers, even when playing or taking food from a child's hand. Reptiles, hedgehogs, and certain types of birds (parrots, for example) may not be permitted due to the potential for biting or the increased risk of transmitting salmonella.

Overcoming the Challenges

Even with the many challenges associated with including animals in the early childhood classroom, 70 percent of study participants believe that classroom pets create a positive learning environment for the children. Some are indifferent to having animals in the classroom, and others think maintaining them is too challenging.

Check national accreditation standards and state licensing guidelines, and consult with veterinarians and other animal specialists, when selecting classroom pets.

The Threat of Salmonella

Salmonella is a bacterium that can be transmitted several ways. When animals are involved, salmonella can be transferred to humans through contaminated water or animal feces. Reptiles, amphibians, snakes, and other animals can be carriers and may transmit salmonella bacteria to humans. Several organizations, including the American Academy of Pediatrics, the Centers for Disease Control and Prevention, and NAEYC, advise not having these animals around children.

One center director from Vermont makes a strong case for the benefits:

> Animals play an important role for many, many reasons. Children are small in the world and have little power of their own. Caring for an animal provides the experience of taking care of a living being even smaller and more vulnerable than they are.
>
> I spent five and a half years working in a day treatment center for dysfunctional families. My part of the program was providing therapeutic care for young children in an early childhood classroom setting. I worked with young children whose stories still make me weep 30 years later. Many of these children had shut down and were unable to let in an adult human being. Yet I saw them lovingly care for the class pets—a guinea pig, rabbit, and hamster. I saw them sit for hours holding, stroking, cuddling, and talking to these animals, telling them the stories that they were unable to share with adults. I would never have a classroom without a pet, even if it was only a fish.

What Are Some Options?

Early childhood educators are creative and resourceful. If, after thoroughly reviewing the considerations, teachers decide not to include a pet as a permanent resident of the classroom, there are still many ways to bring animals into the setting and curriculum.

Projects Based on Animals

Consider the children's interests and the intended learning outcomes when exploring ways to relate animals to the curriculum. In no other story was the children's interest more evident than in this example provided by an early childhood center director in New Mexico:

> I was a kindergarten teacher during 9/11. The children in my classroom expressed an interest in the rescue dogs, so we began a yearlong project on dogs and rescue dogs. The children collected pennies to send to the rescue foundation to support a rescue dog. We took a field trip to the bank to cash in the pennies, then to the post office to mail off the check, and then to the park, where we had a picnic and were visited by a rescue dog team.

Annual Animal Events

Special occasions are great opportunities to safely, and with little investment of resources, include animals in a program. Consider this activity at a private early childhood center in Kentucky:

> We have a pet blessing every October to celebrate St. Francis Day. The children and their families are invited to bring their pets for a blessing from our priest. Various animals

attend this blessing, and it is one of the most fun family activities we offer. It is always very well attended.

And from Texas:

> One year during NAEYC's Week of the Young Child (in April), we asked families to bring in pets and other animals. We sent out a blanket notice to all families about animal visits (addressing allergies and fear of animals, and assuring heavy supervision) and collected current pet vaccination information. All sorts of animals visited. We had one or two days of horses, turtles, dogs, ferrets, lambs, goats, birds, gerbils, pigs, cats, snakes, and so on. It was a lot of fun and excitement for the young children.

Close-ups with Nature

Encouraging natural wildlife such as birds, squirrels, insects, and deer to spend time in the view of the children can lead to numerous teachable moments. Hanging a bird feeder outside a window is an easy way to invite birds. Other ways to incorporate animals in the curriculum include taking field trips to farms or zoos, inviting representatives from zoos or animal shelters to visit the classroom, going on nature hikes, or creating a natural area outside.

In Closing

As the number of animals in early childhood classrooms increases, it is critical that educators of young children provide meaningful interactions between children and animals to enhance classroom experiences. Study participants have shared several considerations for maintaining positive environments for both children and animals. While concerns and benefits vary based on curriculum and behavioral needs, it is clear that including animals in the early childhood classroom has the potential to engage and inspire both educators and young children.

References

Bailie, P.E. 2010. "From the One-Hour Field Trip to a Nature Preschool: Partnering With Environmental Organizations." *Young Children* 65 (4): 76–82.

Dubosarsky, M., B. Murphy, G. Roehrig, L.C. Frost, J. Jones, & S.P. Carlson, with N. Londo, C.J.B. Melchert, C. Gettel, & J. Bement. 2011. "Animosh Tracks on the Playground, Minnows in the Sensory Table: Incorporating Cultural Themes to Promote Preschoolers' Critical Thinking in American Indian Head Start Classrooms." *Young Children* 66 (5): 20–29.

Fine, A.H., ed. 2010. *Handbook on Animal-Assisted Therapy: Theoretical Foundations and Guidelines for Practice.* New York: Academic Press.

Gee, N.R, J.M. Belcher, J.L. Grabski, M. Dejesus, & W. Riley. 2012. "The Presence of a Therapy Dog Results in Improved Object Recognition Performance in Preschool Children." *Anthrozoös* 25 (3): 289–300.

Hachey, A.C., & D. Butler. 2012. "Creatures in the Classroom: Including Insects and Small Animals in Your Preschool Gardening Curriculum." *Young Children 67* (2): 38–42. www.naeyc.org/tyc/files/tyc/file/V5N5/HacheyButler.%20 Creatures%20in%20the%20Class room.pdf

Jackson, J. 2012. "Animal-Assisted Therapy: The Human-Animal Bond in Relation to Human Health and Wellness." Capstone paper, Winona State University. www.winona.edu/ counseloreducation/images/justine_jackson_capstone.pdf

Kwong, M.J., & K. Bartholomew. 2011. "Not Just a Dog: An Attachment Perspective on Relationships With Assistance Dogs." *Attachment & Human Development* 13 (5): 421–36.

Nielson, J.A., & L.A. Delude. 1989. "Behavior of Young Children in the Presence of Different Kinds of Animals." *Anthrozoös* 3 (2): 119–29.

Shaw, D.M. 2013. "Man's Best Friend as a Reading Facilitator." *The Reading Teacher* 66 (5): 365–71. www.therapyanimals. org/Research_&_Results_files/Shaw%20Mans%20Best%20 Friend%20Doogan%201.13.pdf

Torquati, J., with M.M. Gabriel, J. Jones-Branch, & J. Leeper-Miller. 2010. "Environmental Education: A Natural Way to Nurture Children's Development and Learning." *Young Children* 65 (6): 98–104.

Wedl, M., & K. Kotrschal. 2009. "Social and Individual Components of Animal Contact in Preschool Children." *Anthrozoös* 22 (4): 383–96.

Critical Thinking

1. Develop a plan of action you would implement if you decided to have an animal in your classroom serving young children.

2. What life skills would you expect children to gain by interacting with a classroom animal?

3. Share your feelings about having an animal in your classroom. Are those based on experiences you had as a child?

Internet References

Classroom Animals and Pets
   http://www.teacherwebshelf.com/classroompets/HomeTOC.htm
Humane Society
   http://www.humanesociety.org/parents_educators/classroom_pet.html
Massachusetts Society for the Prevention of Cruelty to Animals
   http://www.mspca.org/programs/humane-education/resources-for-educators/animals-in-education/school-policy-on-classroom.html
Pets in the Classroom
   http://www.petsintheclassroom.org/

CLARISSA M. UTTLEY, PhD, is a professor of early childhood studies at Plymouth State University in Plymouth, New Hampshire. Clarissa's research focuses on ethically including animals in early childhood classrooms to support the learning and development of young children.

Article   Prepared by: Karen Menke Paciorek, *Eastern Michigan University*

Food Allergy Concerns in Primary Classrooms

Keeping Children Safe

PEGGY THELEN AND ELIZABETH ANN CAMERON

Learning Outcomes

After reading this article, you will be able to:

- Describe at least three safe food policies.

- Plan ways to include all children in safe and healthy eating environments in a school setting.

Food-allergy awareness and management have only lately come to the forefront in early childhood settings, although advocacy organizations have been working on the issue for more than a decade (FAAN, n.d.). A national poll (C.S. Mott Children's Hospital 2009) asked parents with children in early education settings if they were aware of what their program does to protect children with food allergies. The poll results indicate that more than three-quarters of these parents knew of one or more preventive actions offered in those settings. Of these actions, the ban on treats or food brought from home was the measure cited most frequently. About half of all parents responded that their children's program or school offered staff training specifically for food allergies, with more food allergy plans seen in early childhood programs (56 percent) than in elementary schools (37 percent).

Schools have a legal and ethical responsibility to be prepared for children with food allergies, so organization and implementation of allergy policies and procedures should receive the importance and time they deserve. This article reviews administrative policies and procedures, child development concerns, and classroom realities related to food allergies.

School Policies and Classroom Procedures

Policies that focus on preventing children from consuming or being exposed to food that may trigger allergic reactions often include banning certain foods from the school, a "no sharing" component, or an "exclusion" component (Behrmann 2010). While banning food may seem to be an easy solution, most experts do not recommend this type of action. Such a policy can be difficult for families whose children do not have food allergies, and can create a false sense of security. Sharing or trading food or utensils must be forbidden due to the obvious possible presence of offending allergens. Creating an allergen-free zone, such as a peanut-free table in the cafeteria, is an alternative strategy (Hay, Harper, & Moore 2006).

Emergency preparedness policies for a child with allergies should include the following (Muñoz-Furlong 2003; Behrmann 2010):

- Each child who has an allergy has a medical information file (such as the model provided by the Food Allergy and Anaphylaxis Network, www.foodallergy.org/files/FAAP.pdf) filled out in cooperation with the child's physician. The file outlines the causes of the child's allergic reactions, states what medication should be administered, and includes a photo of the child, a list of emergency contacts, preferred hospital, copies of medical cards, and a list of trained staff members.

- The child's medical information file includes injectable, prefilled intramuscular epinephrine (common brand

Article   Prepared by: Karen Menke Paciorek, *Eastern Michigan University*

Every Child, Every Day

The six elements of effective reading instruction don't require much time or money—just educators' decision to put them in place.

RICHARD L. ALLINGTON AND RACHAEL E. GABRIEL

Learning Outcomes

After reading this article, you will be able to:

- Describe six research-based elements that support reading instruction.

- Explain why child choice is important to the development of early literacy skills.

"Every child a reader" has been the goal of instruction, education research, and reform for at least three decades. We now know more than ever about how to accomplish this goal. Yet few students in the United States regularly receive the best reading instruction we know how to give.

Instead, despite good intentions, educators often make decisions about instruction that compromise or supplant the kind of experiences all children need to become engaged, successful readers. This is especially true for struggling readers, who are much less likely than their peers to participate in the kinds of high-quality instructional activities that would ensure that they learn to read.

Six Elements for Every Child

Here, we outline six elements of instruction that every child should experience every day. Each of these elements can be implemented in any district and any school, with any curriculum or set of materials, and without additional funds. All that's necessary is for adults to make the decision to do it.

1. Every Child Reads Something He or She Chooses

The research base on student-selected reading is robust and conclusive: Students read more, understand more, and are more likely to continue reading when they have the opportunity to choose what they read. In a 2004 meta-analysis, Guthrie and Humenick found that the two most powerful instructional design factors for improving reading motivation and comprehension were (1) student access to many books and (2) personal choice of what to read.

We're not saying that students should never read teacher- or district-selected texts. But at some time every day, they should be able to choose what they read.

The experience of choosing in itself boosts motivation. In addition, offering choice makes it more likely that every reader will be matched to a text that he or she can read well. If students initially have trouble choosing texts that match their ability level and interest, teachers can provide limited choices to guide them toward successful reading experiences. By giving students these opportunities, we help them develop the ability to choose appropriate texts for themselves—a skill that dramatically increases the likelihood they will read outside school (Ivey & Broaddus, 2001, Reis et al., 2007).

Some teachers say they find it difficult to provide a wide selection of texts because of budget constraints. Strangely, there is always money available for workbooks, photocopying, and computers; yet many schools claim that they have no budget for large, multileveled classroom libraries. This is interesting because research has demonstrated that access to self-selected texts improves students' reading performance (Krashen, 2011), whereas no evidence indicates that workbooks, photocopies, or computer tutorial programs have ever done so (Cunningham & Stanovich, 1998; Dynarski, 2007).

There is, in fact, no way they ever could. When we consider that the typical 4th grade classroom has students reading anywhere from the 2nd to the 9th grade reading levels (and that later grades have an even wider range), the idea that one workbook or textbook could meet the needs of every reader is absurd (Hargis, 2006). So, too, is the idea that skills developed through isolated, worksheet-based skills practice and fill-in-the-blank vocabulary quizzes will transfer to real reading in the absence of any evidence that they ever have. If school principals eliminated the budget for workbooks and worksheets and instead spent the money on real books for classroom libraries, this decision could dramatically improve students' opportunities to become better readers.

2. Every Child Reads Accurately

Good readers read with accuracy almost all the time. The last 60 years of research on optimal text difficulty—a body of research that began with Betts (1949)—consistently demonstrates the importance of having students read texts they can read accurately and understand. In fact, research shows that reading at 98 percent or higher accuracy is essential for reading acceleration. Anything less slows the rate of improvement, and anything below 90 percent accuracy doesn't improve reading ability at all (Allington, 2012; Ehri, Dreyer, Flugman, & Gross, 2007).

Although the idea that students read better when they read more has been supported by studies for the last 70 years, policies that simply increase the amount of time allocated for students to read often find mixed results (National Reading Panel, 2000). The reason is simple: It's not just the time spent with a book in hand, but rather the intensity and volume of *high-success* reading, that determines a student's progress in learning to read (Allington, 2009; Kuhn et al., 2006).

When students read accurately, they solidify their word-recognition, decoding, and word-analysis skills. Perhaps more important, they are likely to understand what they read—and, as a result, to enjoy reading.

In contrast, struggling students who spend the same amount of time reading texts that they can't read accurately are at a disadvantage in several important ways. First, they read less text; it's slow going when you encounter many words you don't recognize instantly. Second, struggling readers are less likely to understand (and therefore enjoy) what they read. They are likely to become frustrated when reading these difficult texts and therefore to lose confidence in their word-attack, decoding, or word-recognition skills. Thus, a struggling reader and

a successful reader who engage in the same 15-minute independent reading session do not necessarily receive equivalent practice, and they are likely to experience different outcomes.

Sadly, struggling readers typically encounter a steady diet of too-challenging texts throughout the school day as they make their way through classes that present grade-level material hour after hour. In essence, traditional instructional practices widen the gap between readers.

3. Every Child Reads Something He or She Understands

Understanding what you've read is the goal of reading. But too often, struggling readers get interventions that focus on basic skills in isolation, rather than on reading connected text for meaning. This common misuse of intervention time often arises from a grave misinterpretation of what we know about reading difficulties.

The findings of neurological research are sometimes used to reinforce the notion that some students who struggle to learn to read are simply "wired differently" (Zambo, 2003) and thus require large amounts of isolated basic skills practice. In fact, this same research shows that remediation that emphasizes comprehension can change the structure of struggling students' brains. Keller and Just (2009) used imaging to examine the brains of struggling readers before and after they received 100 hours of remediation—including lots of reading and rereading of real texts. The white matter of the struggling readers was of lower structural quality than that of good readers before the intervention, but it improved following the intervention. And these changes in the structure of the brain's white matter consistently predicted increases in reading ability.

Numerous other studies (Aylward et al., 2003; Krafnick, Flowers, Napoliello, & Eden, 2011; Shaywitz et al., 2004) have supported Keller and Just's findings that comprehensive reading instruction is associated with changed activation patterns that mirror those of typical readers. These studies show that it doesn't take neurosurgery or banging away at basic skills to enable the brain to develop the ability to read: It takes lots of reading and rereading of text that students find engaging and comprehensible.

The findings from brain research align well with what we've learned from studies of reading interventions. Regardless of their focus, target population, or publisher, interventions that accelerate reading development routinely devote at least two-thirds of their time to reading and rereading rather than isolated or contrived skill practice (Allington, 2011). These findings have been consistent for the last 50 years—yet the typical reading intervention used in schools today has struggling readers spending the bulk of their time on tasks other than reading and rereading actual texts.

> **Students read more, understand more, and are more likely to continue reading when they have the opportunity to choose what they read.**

Studies of exemplary elementary teachers further support the finding that more authentic reading develops better readers (Allington, 2002; Taylor, Pearson, Peterson, & Rodriguez, 2003). In these large-scale national studies, researchers found that students in more-effective teachers' classrooms spent a larger percentage of reading instructional time actually reading; students in less-effective teachers' classrooms spent more time using worksheets, answering low-level, literal questions, or completing before-and-after reading activities. In addition, exemplary teachers were more likely to differentiate instruction so that all readers had books they could actually read accurately, fluently, and with understanding.

4. Every Child Writes about Something Personally Meaningful

In our observations in schools across several states, we rarely see students writing anything more than fill-in-the-blank or short-answer responses during their reading block. Those who do have the opportunity to compose something longer than a few sentences are either responding to a teacher-selected prompt or writing within a strict structural formula that turns even paragraphs and essays into fill-in-the-blank exercises.

As adults, we rarely if ever write to a prompt, and we almost never write about something we don't know about. Writing is called *composition* for a good reason: We actually *compose* (construct something unique) when we write. The opportunity to compose continuous text about something meaningful is not just something nice to have when there's free time after a test or at the end of the school year. Writing provides a different modality within which to practice the skills and strategies of reading for an authentic purpose.

When students write about something they care about, they use conventions of spelling and grammar because it matters to them that their ideas are communicated, not because they will lose points or see red ink if they don't (Cunningham & Cunningham, 2010). They have to think about what words will best convey their ideas to their readers. They have to encode these words using letter patterns others will recognize. They have to make sure they use punctuation in a way that will help their readers understand which words go together, where a thought starts and ends, and what emotion goes with it. They have to think about what they know about the structure of similar texts to set up their page and

organize their ideas. This process is especially important for struggling readers because it produces a comprehensible text that the student can read, reread, and analyze.

5. Every Child Talks with Peers about Reading and Writing

Research has demonstrated that conversation with peers improves comprehension and engagement with texts in a variety of settings (Cazden, 1988). Such literary conversation does not focus on recalling or retelling what students read. Rather, it asks students to analyze, comment, and compare—in short, to think about what they've read. Fall, Webb, and Chudowsky (2000) found better outcomes when kids simply talked with a peer about what they read than when they spent the same amount of class time highlighting important information after reading.

Similarly, Nystrand (2006) reviewed the research on engaging students in literate conversations and noted that even small amounts of such conversation (10 minutes a day) improved standardized test scores, regardless of students' family background or reading level. Yet struggling readers were the least likely to discuss daily what they read with peers. This was often because they were doing extra basic-skills practice instead. In class discussions, struggling readers were more likely to be asked literal questions about what they had read, to prove they "got it," rather than to be engaged in a conversation about the text.

Time for students to talk about their reading and writing is perhaps one of the most underused, yet easy-to-implement, elements of instruction. It doesn't require any special materials, special training, or even large amounts of time. Yet it provides measurable benefits in comprehension, motivation, and even language competence. The task of switching between writing, speaking, reading, and listening helps students make connections between, and thus solidify, the skills they use in each. This makes peer conversation especially important for English language learners, another population that we rarely ask to talk about what they read.

6. Every Child Listens to a Fluent Adult Read Aloud

Listening to an adult model fluent reading increases students' own fluency and comprehension skills (Trelease, 2001), as well as expanding their vocabulary, background knowledge, sense of story, awareness of genre and text structure, and comprehension of the texts read (Wu & Samuels, 2004).

Yet few teachers above 1st grade read aloud to their students every day (Jacobs, Morrison, & Swinyard, 2000). This high-impact, low-input strategy is another underused component of the kind of instruction that supports readers. We categorize it as low-input because, once again, it does not require special materials or training; it simply requires a decision to use class time more effectively. Rather than conducting whole-class reading of a single text that fits few readers, teachers should choose to spend a few minutes a day reading to their students.

Things That Really Matter

Most of the classroom instruction we have observed lacks these six research-based elements. Yet it's not difficult to find the time and resources to implement them. Here are a few suggestions.

First, eliminate almost all worksheets and workbooks. Use the money saved to purchase books for classroom libraries; use the time saved for self-selected reading, self-selected writing, literary conversations, and read-alouds.

Second, ban test-preparation activities and materials from the school day. Although sales of test preparation materials provide almost two-thirds of the profit that testing companies earn (Glovin & Evans, 2006), there are no studies demonstrating that engaging students in test prep ever improved their reading proficiency—or even their test performance (Guthrie, 2002). As with eliminating workbook completion, eliminating test preparation provides time and money to spend on the things that really matter in developing readers.

It's time for the elements of effective instruction described here to be offered more consistently to every child, in every school, every day. Remember, adults have the power to make these decisions; kids don't. Let's decide to give them the kind of instruction they need.

First, eliminate almost all worksheets and workbooks.

References

Allington, R. L. (2002). What I've learned about effective reading instruction from a decade of studying exemplary elementary classroom teachers. *Phi Delta Kappan, 83*(10), 740–747.

Allington, R. L. (2009). If they don't read much . . . 30 years later. In E. H. Hiebert (Ed.), *Reading more, reading better* (pp. 30–54). New York: Guilford.

Allington, R. L. (2011). Research on reading/learning disability interventions. In S. J. Samuels & A. E. Farstrup (Eds.), *What research has to say about reading instruction* (4th ed., pp. 236–265). Newark, DE: International Reading Association.

Allington, R. L. (2012). *What really matters for struggling readers: Designing research-based programs* (3rd ed.). Boston: Allyn and Bacon.

Aylward, E. H., Richards, T. L., Berninger, V. W., Nagy, W. E, Field, K. M., Grimme, A. C., Richards, A. L., Thomson, J. B., & Cramer, S. C. (2003). Instructional treatment associated with changes in brain activation in children with dyslexia. *Neurology, 61*(2), E5–6.

Betts, E. A. (1949). Adjusting instruction to individual needs. In N. B. Henry (Ed.), *The forty-eighth yearbook of the National Society for the Study of Education: Part II, Reading in the elementary school* (pp. 266–283). Chicago: University of Chicago Press.

Cazden, C. B. (1988). *Classroom discourse: The language of teaching and learning.* Portsmouth, NH: Heinemann.

Cunningham, A. E., & Stanovich, K. E. (1998). The impact of print exposure on word recognition. In J. Metsala & L. Ehri (Eds.), *Word recognition in beginning literacy* (pp. 235–262). Mahwah, NJ: Erlbaum.

Cunningham, P. M., & Cunningham, J. W. (2010). *What really matters in writing: Research-based practices across the elementary curriculum.* Boston: Allyn and Bacon.

Dynarski, M. (2007). *Effectiveness of reading and mathematics software products: Findings from the first student cohort.* Washington, DC: Institute for Education Sciences, U.S. Department of Education. Retrieved from http://ies.ed.gov/ncee/pubs/20074005.

Ehri, L. C., Dreyer, L. G., Flugman, B., & Gross, A. (2007). Reading Rescue: An effective tutoring intervention model for language minority students who are struggling readers in first grade. *American Educational Research Journal, 44*(2), 414–448.

Fall, R., Webb, N. M., & Chudowsky, N. (2000). Group discussion and large-scale language arts assessment: Effects on students' comprehension. *American Educational Research Journal, 37*(4), 911–941.

Glovin, D., & Evans, D. (2006, December). How test companies fail your kids. *Bloomberg Markets,* 127–138. Retrieved from http://timeoutfromtesting.org/bloomberg_education.pdf.

Guthrie, J. T. (2002). Preparing students for high-stakes test taking in reading. In A. Farstrup & S. J. Samuels (Eds.), *What research has to say about reading instruction* (pp. 370–391). Newark, DE: International Reading Association.

Guthrie, J. T., & Humenick, N. M. (2004). Motivating students to read: Evidence for classroom practices that increase motivation and achievement. In P. McCardle & V. Chhabra (Eds.), *The voice of evidence in reading research* (pp. 329–354). Baltimore: Paul Brookes.

Hargis, C. (2006). Setting standards: An exercise in futility? *Phi Delta Kappan, 87*(5), 393–395.

Ivey, G., & Broaddus, K. (2001). Just plain reading: A survey of what makes students want to read in middle schools. *Reading Research Quarterly, 36,* 350–377.

Jacobs, J. S., Morrison, T. G., & Swinyard, W. R. (2000). Reading aloud to students: A national probability study of classroom reading practices of elementary school teachers. *Reading Psychology, 21*(3), 171–193.

Keller, T. A., & Just, M. A. (2009). Altering cortical activity: Remediation-induced changes in the white matter of poor readers. *Neuron, 64*(5), 624–631.

Krafnick, A. J., Flowers, D. L., Napoliello, E. M., & Eden, G. F. (2011). Gray matter volume changes following reading intervention in dyslexic children. *Neuroimage, 57*(3), 733–741.

Krashen, S. (2011). *Free voluntary reading.* Santa Barbara, CA: Libraries Unlimited.

Kuhn, M. R., Schwanenflugel, P., Morris, R. D., Morrow, L. M., Woo, D., Meisinger, B., et al. (2006). Teaching children to become fluent and automatic readers. *Journal of Literacy Research, 38*(4), 357–388.

National Reading Panel. (2000). *Teaching children to read: An evidence-based assessment of the scientific research literature on reading and its implications for reading instruction.* Rockville, MD: National Institutes of Child Health and Human Development. Retrieved from www.nationalreadingpanel.org/publications/summary.htm.

Nystrand, M. (2006). Research on the role of classroom discourse as it affects reading comprehension. *Research in the Teaching of English, 40,* 392–412.

Reis, S. M., McCoach, D. B., Coyne, M., Schreiber, F. J., Eckert, R. D., & Gubbins, E. J. (2007). Using planned enrichment strategies with direct instruction to improve reading fluency, comprehension, and attitude toward reading: An evidence-based study. *Elementary School Journal, 108*(1), 3–24.

Shaywitz, B., Shaywitz, S., Blachman, B., Pugh, K., Fulbright, R. K., Skudlarski, P., et al. (2004). Development of left occiptotemporal systems for skilled reading in children after phonologically based intervention. *Biological Psychiatry, 55*(9), 926–933.

Taylor, B. M., Pearson, P. D., Peterson, D. S., & Rodriguez, M. C. (2003). Reading growth in high-poverty classrooms: The influence of teacher practices that encourage cognitive engagement in literacy learning. *Elementary School Journal, 104,* 3–28.

Trelease, J. (2001). *Read-aloud handbook* (5th ed.). New York: Viking-Penguin.

Wu, Y., & Samuels, S. J. (2004, May). *How the amount of time spent on independent reading affects reading achievement.* Paper presented at the annual convention of the International Reading Association, Reno, Nevada.

Zambo, D. (2003). The importance of providing scientific information to children with dyslexia. *Dyslexia* [online magazine]. Retrieved from Dyslexia Parents Resource at www.dyslexia-parent.com/mag47.html.

Critical Thinking

1. Teach a writing mini-lesson that focuses on a self-selected text that the child can write about. Observe the connections that suggest comprehension between what was written and what was read.

2. Visit a classroom with a large classroom library. Observe the order of the texts, the accessibility by the students, and the kinds of books that the teacher has in her library.

Internet References

Common Core State Standards Initiative
www.corestandards.org

Grade Level Reading Lists
www.gradelevelreadinglists.org

International Children's Digital Library
http://en.childrenslibrary.org/index.shtml

International Reading Association
www.reading.org

RICHARD L. ALLINGTON is a professor at the University of Tennessee in Knoxville; richardallington@aol.com.

RACHAEL E. GABRIEL is assistant professor at the University of Connecticut in Storrs; rachael.gabriel@uconn.edu.

Allington, Richard L.; Gabriel, Rachael E. From *Educational Leadership*, March 2012, pp. 10–15. Copyright ©2012 by ASCD. Reprinted by permission. The Association for Supervision and Curriculum Development is a worldwide community of educators advocating sound policies and sharing best practices to achieve the success of each learner. To learn more, visit ASCD at www.ascd.org.